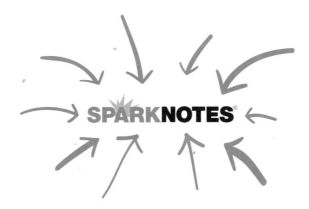

SPARKNOTES®

ILLUSTRaTED
VOCABULARY

SPARK PUBL

D1315790

© 2008 by Spark Publishing

All rights reserved. No part of this publication may be reproduced, stored in a retrieval system, or transmitted, in any form or by any means, electronic, mechanical, photocopying, recording, or otherwise, without prior written permission from the publisher.

Illustrations by Dan O. Williams

SPARKNOTES is a registered trademark of SparkNotes LLC.

Spark Publishing
A Division of Barnes & Noble
120 Fifth Avenue
New York, NY 10011
www.sparknotes.com

ISBN-13: 978-1-4114-0320-8
ISBN-10: 1-4114-0320-7

Library of Congress Cataloging-in Publication Data available upon request.

Please submit changes or report errors to www.sparknotes.com/errors.

Printed and bound in China

10 9 8 7 6 5 4 3 2 1

Acknowledgments

Many people at SparkNotes helped to make this book possible and (we hope you agree) great. Lindsay Weiskittel, our tireless editor, provided patient feedback and wrangled our sentences and schedules with aplomb. We are grateful for her hard work and dedication. Our many thanks go out to Laurie Barnett for pitching us this idea in the first place, and for showing us the publishing ropes. Liz Kessler's investigative skills and sharp wit have been invaluable. Thanks to Alysha Bullock for final shepherding.

We must also offer a hearty thank you to our families in Arizona and New York, who supported and encouraged us as we worked together in life and on the page.

Contents

Introduction

A strong vocabulary is important to everyone. It not only allows you to communicate more effectively and accurately but also makes you sound smarter and more polished. A high-level vocabulary can also get you jobs, respect—even dates. More important, it can raise your score on exams such as the SAT, ACT, and other standardized tests.

Whatever your reason for wanting to expand your vocabulary, this book can help. You'll walk away having learned and memorized 250 new words—and you'll have done it painlessly. You might even have some fun! And it's all because of the power of mnemonics.

What's a Mnemonic?

Mnemonic (nuh-MON-ik) is just a fancy way of saying "memory aid." A mnemonic usually takes the form of a short, easily memorized saying. You probably already use several of them in your daily life. Play an instrument? You might have learned the musical scale by memorizing this handy saying: **E**very **G**ood **B**oy **D**eserves **F**un. Maybe you mutter "righty-tighty, lefty-loosey" whenever you have to fix something with a wrench, or maybe you recite "*I* before *E* except after *C*" whenever you have to spell *receive* or *believe*. These are all examples of common mnemonics. (Try saying that ten times fast!)

The Power of Mnemonics

We created this book because we felt there should be an easier way to learn vocabulary. Because let's face it: Life is too short to sit around memorizing word lists! We started with 250 difficult vocabulary words that are commonly found on the SAT and other standardized exams. Then we created a unique, mnemonics-based learning system around those words to help you learn and truly *memorize* their meanings. We use a variety of components to make these new words and their definitions stick: everything from rhythm and rhyme to humor and dynamic illustrations. So now, studying vocab won't just be more effective—it'll actually be fun!

Ride the power of mnemonics to a better, stronger vocabulary with *SparkNotes Illustrated Vocabulary*.

How to Use This Book

This book uses multiple tactics to help you understand, learn, and memorize 250 new words. Each page has five components that work in concert to make sure each new word sticks—and sticks firmly.

1. The Vocabulary Word, including its pronunciation, part of speech, and definition.

tome tohm (*n.*) a large book

2. The Mnemonic Phrase, a rhyming sentence that allows you to quickly and easily memorize both the vocabulary word and its definition. Don't blame us if you start walking around the house chanting these sentences to yourself—that's the point! They're sing-songy and silly so that you remember them easily.

The tiny _gnome_ read a giant _tome_.

3. The Sound Links, words or phrases that sound like the vocabulary word. Sometimes the link rhymes with the original word; sometimes it rhymes and shares other sound similarities.

The tiny _gnome_ read a giant _tome_.

Here the sound link, gnome, is a simple rhyme.

Con, Viv, and Al are _convivial_ pals.

Here the sound links (*Con, Viv,* and *Al*) share sound similarities as well.

4. The Illustration drives the mnemonic home. If you're a better visual learner than you are an auditory learner (that is, someone who learns through sounds), the illustration will help trigger your memory when you have to recall the word's definition.

5. Three sample sentences further clarify the word's meaning and show you how the word may be used in different contexts.

- The dusty *tome* had become a permanent fixture on his desk, like an overgrown paperweight.
- Stuffed with various pre-med *tomes*, Renee's backpack very likely outweighed her.
- Perched on a pedestal in the corner of the library with an old magnifying glass at its side, the unabridged dictionary seemed an imposing *tome*.

You can flip through this book randomly, stopping at pages that catch your eye and learning the words on that page. But if you want to be more disciplined about it—if you're bulking up your vocab for a test, for example—work through the words in the order they're presented. After every group of ten words, you'll see the following two drills:

1. Refresh Your Memory. Here you'll match the term with the correct definition.

2. Test Your Knowledge. This drill is a series of fill-in-the-blank sentences.

After working through a set of words, try one of the exercises. Score well? Try the next one. Score lower than you'd like? Go back and review the words in question, then test yourself again with the second exercise.

However you decide to use this book, you're sure to end up with a wider, more sophisticated vocabulary. So what are you waiting for? Turn the page and start memorizing with mnemonics!

abate

uh-BEYT (*v.*) to reduce, lessen

The picky wife's nagging would eventually *abate* when her distracted husband learned not to be _late_.

— Genevieve's enthusiasm *abated* when Richard told her the ride to New York would be more than seven hours long.

— When the storm finally *abated*, the children rushed outside to inhale the thick, chalky smell of ozone lingering in the air.

— The ache in Elena's right elbow *abated* after some icing and two ibuprofens.

abdicate

AB-di-keyt **(v.)** to give up a position, usually one of leadership

Elderly *Abe dictates* that he'll *abdicate* his position as the master of the kitchen.

— The senile king finally agreed to *abdicate* the throne after a long battle with his court.
— Kelly *abdicated* as secretary of the Bubblegum Club when she got her braces.
— After the newspapers reported on the scandal, the CEO was forced to *abdicate*.

abet

uh-BET **(v.)** to aid, help, encourage

The dealer never should *abet*
a cheat who's there to place *a bet*.

- Maynard could not agree to *abet* his father-in-law with such suspicious bookkeeping.
- The defendant was eventually charged with aiding and *abetting* the murderer.
- Charlie needed someone to *abet* him with his homework, or else he would ignore it altogether.

abject

AB-jekt *(adj.)* wretched, pitiful

**"To this punishment I must <u>*object*</u>!
Putting hyper Georgie in the corner is too *abject*!"**

— When she declined his offer of marriage, he descended into an
abject depression.
— The family lived in *abject* poverty, subsisting on handouts from a
local charity.
— Puppy mills are notorious for their inhumane, *abject* conditions.

abrogate

AB-ruh-geyt **(v.)** to abolish, usually by authority

The senior class president wants to *abrogate* **the no-baseball-caps rule that his** *brothers hate*.

— The principal temporarily *abrogated* the students' right to freedom of speech after someone wore a T-shirt emblazoned with an expletive.

— City Council voted to *abrogate* the leash law in local parks, so dogs can now run free within park boundaries.

— The landlord threatened to *abrogate* the lease agreement after the tenant painted the apartment hot pink.

acrimony

AK-ruh-moh-nee **(n.)** bitterness, discord

Acres of money **caused** *acrimony*
between the two honeys.

— The young woman spoke of her ex-boyfriend through a filter of *acrimony* and tears.
— The owner of the independent book shop felt a great deal of *acrimony* toward the giant corporate bookseller on the next block.
— Pam thought her cat would never get over its *acrimony* for her dog, but one day she found them napping together on the couch.

advocate

1. AD-vuh-keyt (*v.*) to argue in favor of something
2. AD-vuh-kit (*n.*) a person who argues in favor of something

**The *avocado* fights for what's right
and *advocates* for vegetable rights.**

— He *advocated* better treatment for factory workers in Guatemala.
— Deb would always be an *advocate* for the simplest, most elegant solution, particularly if she was involved in its design.
— Ralph Nader's career as a consumer *advocate* began with his examination of the safety of automobiles.

agile

AJ-ayhl (*adj.*) quick, nimble

**It took awhile to swim to _Aggie's isles_,
but since she's _agile_, it only took a wink and a smile.**

- After only a month of yoga practice, Fern could feel her body becoming more *agile*.
- Though she was nearing ninety-five, her mind was sharp and *agile*.
- Though they don't have nine lives, cats are known for their *agile* movements, which often keep them from injuring themselves.

aisle

ahyl (**n.**) a passageway between rows of seats

Jeff had his seat on the *aisle*, so he missed the view of the River *Nile*.

— Barry found everything he needed for Thanksgiving dinner in the frozen food *aisle*.

— Sally saw Chuck with the preacher at the end of the *aisle* and thought, "I can't go through with this."

— The gospel choir had the whole congregation singing and dancing in the *aisles*.

alleviate

uh–LEE-vee-eyt **(v.)** to relieve, make more bearable

All evening we ate, so we could *alleviate*
the pain of listening to Becky's boring new mate.

— A gentle massage can help *alleviate* stress and muscle tension.
— Dave slept with a small nightlight to *alleviate* his fear of the dark.
— The ibuprofen she took did nothing to *alleviate* the searing pain of her headache, but two Bloody Marys did the trick.

DRILL 1

Refresh Your Memory

Match the word and link to its corresponding definition.

1. abate (late)
2. abdicate (Abe dictates)
3. abet (a bet)
4. abject (object
5. abrogate (brothers hate)
6. acrimony (acres of money)
7. advocate (avocado)
8. agile (Aggie's isles)
9. aisle (Nile)
10. alleviate (all evening we ate)

A. bitterness, dischord
B. to abolish, usually by authority
C. quick, nimble
D. to reduce, lessen
E. to relieve, make more bearable
F. wretched, pitiful
G. a passageway between rows of seats
H. to aid, help, encourage
I. to give up a position, usually one of leadership
J. to argue in favor of something

Test Your Knowledge

Fill in the blanks with the correct word from the list above. Some word forms may need changing.

1. The rain poured down for a while, then _____.

2. Though they vowed that no girl would ever come between them, Biff and Trevor could not keep _____ from overwhelming their friendship after they both fell in love with Teresa.

3. When he realized that the revolutionaries would surely win, the king _____ his throne.

4. This drug will _____ the symptoms of the terrible disease, but only for a while.

5. The Bill of Rights assures that the government cannot _____ our right to a free press.

6. The spy succeeded only because he had a friend on the inside to _____ him.

7. The dogs were too slow to catch the _____ rabbit.

8. After losing all her money, falling into a puddle, and breaking her ankle, Eloise was _____.

9. Arnold _____ turning left at the stop sign, even though everyone else thought we should turn right.

10. Once we got inside the stadium, we walked down the _____ to our seats.

allocate

AL-oh-kayt **(v.)** to distribute, set aside

**" *'Allo, Cate*! Would you *allocate*
some cookies for your Aussie mate?"**

— The Boy Scouts *allocated* rations for a weeklong camping trip,
— The tasks were *allocated* among the advanced and intermediate
workers.
— Charities in New York *allocate* over 5 million dollars a year to
battle homelessness.

ambiguous

am–BIG-yoo-uhs (*adj.*) uncertain, variably interpretable

The pig farmer was *ambiguous* about his *ham's bigness*.

— The blinking red light seemed *ambiguous* to Shani, so she drove through the intersection without stopping.
— Dale shrugged *ambiguously* when Katie asked him what he wanted to do Friday night.
— Antonio's mother gave an *ambiguous* answer when he asked her whether she'd smoked in college.

ameliorate

a–MEE–yuh–luh–rate **(*v.*) to improve, make better**

Carol would pay *a million* bucks cash to *ameliorate* her terrible rash.

— There was nothing she could do to *ameliorate* the terrible situation, and her constant apologies rang hollow to everyone involved.

— The young activist believed that he could *ameliorate* human suffering with bold new ideas about social change.

— In an effort to *ameliorate* the disagreement, Jeff proposed a compromise to which everyone begrudgingly agreed.

amorphous

uh-MAWR-fuhs (*adj.*) without definite shape or type

Students, I'm sad to say these sculptures **are even crappier** than your first ones!

The picky art teacher _made more_ of a _fuss_ when his students' sculptures were dull and _amorphous_.

— His latest painting consisted of *amorphous* orange blobs and harsh purple triangles.
— Larissa could see the *amorphous* shapes of jelly fish and the pale legs of other swimmers underwater.
— No matter how much she exercised, Martha's body seemed *amorphous*, and never as lithe or muscular as she'd hoped.

analgesic

an-l-JEE-zik **(n.)** something that reduces pain

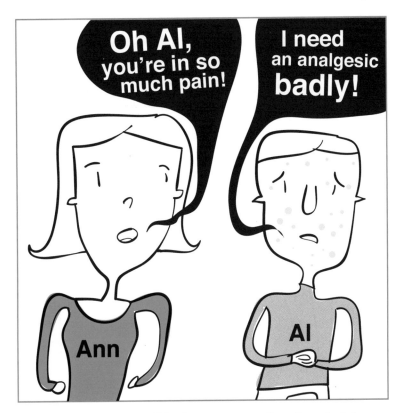

Ann said *"Al, jeez*, you look *sick*!
Take an *analgesic* so you don't look so *ick*!"

— The *analgesic* effect of the martinis Glen had at lunch made it
so that he felt nothing when he stubbed his toe walking back to
the office.

— Noah wished desperately for an *analgesic* for his broken heart.

— The doctor prescribed a strong *analgesic* after his patient broke
her ankle in particularly lively game of backyard basketball.

anesthesia

an-uhs-THEE-zhuh (*n.*) loss of sensation

It doesn't matter how high nurse _Annie's fees are_,
you don't want surgery without her *anesthesia*.

— His liberal intake of alcohol acted as a kind of *anesthesia* to his
depressing and often painful life.

— The *anesthesia* in her lower abdomen meant that Katie barely
blinked as the doctors removed her appendix.

— Clark found that he'd developed *anesthesia* in his backside after
sitting in the grass at an outdoor concert all afternoon.

anomaly

uh-NOM-uh-lee **(n.)** something that does not fit
into the normal order

**The two-headed flowers grew _abnormally_—
but the fact that they spoke was the true _anomaly_.**

- The Gilroys' black-haired child was an _anomaly_ in the mostly redheaded Irish family.
- New Yorkers like to think that the Yankees' 2006 World Series defeat was just an _anomaly_.
- The dog's green eyes were an _anomaly_ for the breed and disqualified him from being shown.

antagonism

an–TAG–uh–niz–uhm (*n.*) hostility

**His *antagonism* caused an *angry schism*:
He had so much anger, no one could come near him.**

— Before she met him at a public event, Anna felt *antagonism* toward the senatorial candidate.

— Our childhood dog had *antagonism* toward all four-legged creatures, except horses, which he happily followed through the meadows near our house.

— The algebra teacher was known for her impossible tests and *antagonism* toward students.

antediluvian

ant-tee-di-LOO-vee-uhn (*adj.*) ancient

**The old *Peruvian ruins*
are *antediluvian*.**

— Priscilla felt her father's ideas about dating were *antediluvian*.
— The archaeology students found *antediluvian* currency strewn around the burial site.
— Though he maintained some *antediluvian* prejudices about city life, the old farmer finally visited his daughter in Toronto.

anxiety

ang-ZAHY-i-tee **(n.)** intense uneasiness

**Chubby _Ann diets with tea_,
but her increasing waistline gives her _anxiety_.**

— Jenny's _anxiety_ about the test was so extreme she was unable to eat breakfast.

— At his weekly breakfast meeting, the mayor professed _anxiety_ over the state of the ancient transit system.

— Dwight felt a rush of _anxiety_ as the vicious dog lunged toward him.

DRILL 2

Refresh Your Memory

Match the word and link to its corresponding definition.

1. allocate ('allo, Cate)
2. ambiguous (ham's bigness)
3. ameliorate (a million)
4. amorphous (made more ... fuss)
5. analgesic (Ann ... Al, jeez ... sick)
6. anesthesia (Annie's fees are)
7. anomaly (abnormally)
8. antagonism (angry schism)
9. antediluvian (Peruvian ruins)
10. anxiety (Ann diets with tea)

A. ancient
B. uncertain, variably interpretable
C. something that reduces pain
D. to improve, make better
E. to distribute, set aside
F. intense uneasiness
G. loss of sensation
H. without definite shape or type
I. something that does not fit into the normal order
J. hostility

Test Your Knowledge

Fill in the blanks with the correct word from the list above. Some word forms may need changing.

1. When the nerves in his spine were damaged, Mr. Hollins suffered _____ in his legs.

2. The effort was doomed from the start, because the reasons behind it were so _____ and hard to pin down.

3. The _____ man still believed that Eisenhower was president of the United States and that hot dogs cost a nickel.

4. The tense situation was _____ when Sam proposed a solution everyone could agree upon.

5. The mayor _____ 30 percent of the funds to improving the town's schools.

6. "That rip in the space-time continuum is certainly a spatial _____," said Spock to Captain Kirk.

7. When he heard about the car crash, he felt _____, because he knew that his girlfriend had been driving on the road where the accident occurred.

8. Put this _____ on the wound so that the poor man feels at least a little better.

9. Superman and Bizarro Superman shared a mutual _____ and often fought.

10. Some people think Caesar married Cleopatra for her power, while others believe he was charmed by her beauty. His actual reasons are _____.

arbiter

AHR-bi-ter **(*n.*)** one who can resolve a
dispute, make a decision

When *Artie bit her*, Patty got mad.
So an *arbiter* made it even and had him wear plaid.

— The twins' mother was tired of acting as *arbiter* of their constant
petty arguments.

— Diplomatic to the core, Chelsea appointed herself *arbiter* of all
office spats.

— The Friday evening cocktail party was attended by designers,
artists, magazine editors, and other *arbiters* of fashion.

arboreal

ar–BORE–ee–al **(adj.) of or relating to trees**

Curious Marge was *arboreal*, **a monkey living in the trees, but she was also an** *arty bore, really*! **She liked painting rocks for fees.**

— The artist's sculptures were *arboreal* and even incorporated tree bark.
— Because it comes from the resin of conifer trees, amber is often called the "*arboreal* gold."
— David was so tall; when he stretched his arms out he seemed *arboreal*.

archetypal

AR-ki-tahy-puhl **(v.) the most representative or typical example of something**

Indiana Jones found the *archetypal* *arch type* **on a trip to Nepal.**

— Everyone in town considered Nathan the *archetypal* nice guy, but no women would date him.
— They had the *archetypal* Victorian home, complete with gas lighting and a parlor.
— Many works of modern literature feature an *archetypal* character like Odysseus.

ardor

AHR-der **(adj.)** extreme vigor, energy, enthusiasm

On the field, Stephanie's team spirit and *ardor* made her able to kick the ball *harder*.

— When Bianca spoke about Picasso's paintings, it was with *ardor* and great passion.

— He lay awake on his thin mattress, watching the blinking neon sign outside his window, filled with *ardor* for the day to come.

— I could admire the *ardor* Brandon felt for his work, but I couldn't match it.

ascertain

AS-er-teyn **(v.)** to perceive, learn

A certain **flea can** *ascertain*
where to make a home in a horse's mane.

— The treasurer must *ascertain* whether funding is available for the park renewal project.

— Carly *ascertained* from her brother's guilty expression that he had once again been reading her diary.

— Using an old map and a compass, Joey tried to *ascertain* where the buried treasure was located.

atone

uh-TOHN **(v.)** to repent, make amends

The apologetic band leader had to *atone* **for playing off-key and singing** *off tone*.

— The church instilled in Molly a need to *atone* for all her mistakes.
— To *atone* for his inadequacies, the husband bought his wife the largest bouquet he could find at the gas station.
— The jury agreed: The criminal must *atone* for his crimes.

attribute

1. uh-TRIB-yoot **(n.)** to credit, assign
2. A-truh-byoot **(v.)** a facet or trait

**Intelligent Trish received _a tribute_
for her smarty-pants _attributes_.**

— The king _attributed_ his downfall to the jester's unfunny jokes.
— Speed and power were the team's greatest _attributes_.
— He _attributed_ the quote to Oscar Wilde, but it had been said first by Leo Tolstoy.

augment

awg-MENT (*v.*) to add to, expand

Auggie meant **to feed the fish,**
but he *augmented* the food with worms and
served it on a dish!

— Donald *augmented* his allowance by collecting change from
under the couch cushions.

— The chef *augments* the chicken broth with a little pepper and
thyme.

— The arrival of a new baby brother *augmented* tensions between
the two older siblings.

aversion

uh–VUR–zhun **(n.)** a particular dislike for something

Victor has an *aversion* that is very strong to *a version* of a song that goes on too long.

— Stuart had a strong *aversion* to work and was fired from nearly every job he had ever held.

— Her deep-seated *aversion* to cats didn't stop at *felis domesticus*; it also included lions, tigers, panthers, leopards, and cheetahs.

— The quiet townspeople had an *aversion* to the obnoxious city folk who flocked to their beautiful seaside village every summer.

behemoth

beh–HEE–muth (*n.*) something of tremendous power or size

Be he moth **or be he man,**
no *behemoth* **monster may attack the land.**

— The community banded together to fight off the corporate *behemoths* and support local business.
— Lexi's truck was *behemoth* and unwieldy, so she traded it in for a bicycle.
— Even as a puppy, Bob's Great Dane Bosco was *behemoth*.

DRILL 3

Refresh Your Memory

Match the word and link to its corresponding definition.

1. arbiter (Artie bit her)
2. arboreal (arty bore, really)
3. archetypal (arch type)
4. ardor (harder)
5. ascertain (a certain)
6. atone (off tone)
7. attribute (a tribute)
8. augment (Auggie meant)
9. aversion (a version)
10. behemoth (be he moth)

A. a facet or trait
B. to repent, make amends
C. to add to, expand
D. of or relating to trees
E. a particular dislike for something
F. one who can resolve a dispute, make a decision
G. something of tremendous power or size
H. extreme vigor, energy, enthusiasm
I. to perceive, learn
J. the most representative or typical example of something

Test Your Knowledge

Fill in the blanks with the correct word from the list above. Some word forms may need changing.

1. He _____ all of his success to his mother's undying encouragement.

2. With a bit of research, the student _____ that some plants can live for weeks without water.

3. The soldiers conveyed their _____ with impassioned battle cries.

4. The new aircraft carrier is among several _____ that the Air Force has added to its fleet.

5. Leaves, roots, and bark are a few _____ traits.

6. The eager student seeks to _____ his knowledge of French vocabulary by reading French literature.

7. The man _____ for forgetting his wife's birthday by buying her five dozen roses.

8. Some believe George Washington, with his flowing white hair and commanding stature, was the _____ politician.

9. The divorce court judge will serve as the _____ between the estranged couple.

10. Because he's from Hawaii, Ben has an _____ to cold climates.

benign

bi-NAHYN (*adj.*) favorable, not threatening, mild

**The child obviously read _Ben's sign_:
It said the tigers were friendly and _benign_.**

— The nurse's _benign_ bedside manner put even the sickest patients at ease.

— Betsy offered a _benign_ smile as she plucked the last cookie from the cookie tray.

— His stage fright melted away as he gazed out on the _benign_ faces in the audience.

berate

bee-RAYT **(v.)** to scold vehemently

The horror director was *berated*
when his film was *G-rated*.

— The babysitter *berated* her charge for spilling his grape juice on her new cashmere sweater.

— Angela's furious boss *berated* her for coming in late all week.

— The mechanic *berated* his client for attempting to run the bus on discarded french fry oil.

blandish

BLAN-dish **(v.)** to coax by using flattery

**The _bland dish_ was of nothing to boast,
but Rita smiled and ate it to _blandish_ her host.**

— The concert was sold out, but Suzanne was able to _blandish_ the bouncer to let her into the VIP section free of charge.

— Raquel figured she could _blandish_ her fiancé into wearing a tuxedo to their wedding.

— The idea of _blandishing_ his supervisor disgusted him, but it was the only way he could get next Friday off.

calumny

CAL-um-nee **(n.)** an attempt to spoil someone else's reputation by spreading lies

Cal admitted *glumly*
that he was the source of the *calumny*.

— The article was considered by most Democrats to be a *calumny* of the newly elected president.

— Dan's *calumny* of his ex-girlfriend didn't convince anyone; in fact, she was as popular as ever.

— Throughout high school, Tricia maintained her popularity with alternating use of *calumny* and flattery.

cajole

kuh-JOHL (*v.*) to urge, coax

When his older sister went to *call Joel*, he tried to *cajole* her to search for his troll.

— The salesman flashed a smile packed with yellowing teeth and *cajoled* his customer into buying a vacuum.

— David has an unnerving ability to *cajole* women into treating him to dinner.

— The children whined and *cajoled* until their father finally agreed to take them out for ice cream.

catalog

KAT-l-og **1. (*v.*) to list, enter into a list**
2. (*n.*) a list or collection

The *cattle log* was a *catalog* of cows that got stuck in the cattle bog.

— Joanie *cataloged* her favorite blogs.

— Justin's vast *catalog* of MP3s threatened to overtake his hard drive.

— The student-teacher mentally *cataloged* the students' faces before calling them by name.

catalyze

KAT-l-ahyz **(v.)** to charge, inspire

The encouraging look in her _cattle's eyes_
would _catalyze_ **Chris to win the livestock prize.**

— The cheerleaders were sent out to _catalyze_ a win for the home
  team.
— Jason's writing was _catalyzed_ by his recent discovery of the
  works of Raymond Carver.
— The goal of the business was to _catalyze_ investments in socially
  responsible companies.

cavort

kuh-VAWRT **(v.) to leap about, behave boisterously**

**The merry little elf is really one to *cavort*;
he dances in his <u>cave</u> with his ogre friend, <u>Ort</u>.**

— The young lambs *cavorted* in the tall grass, oblivious to their fate as Easter dinner.

— At nearly forty years old, Matilda wasn't often seen *cavorting* around like a youngster, but she had to make an exception when she saw her joyful nieces.

— Josiah spent every weekend *cavorting* with models and rock stars in exclusive clubs all over the city.

chastise

chas–TAHYZ (*v.*) to criticize severely

**The wife *chastised* her husband's buys
and his purchase of the wrong *chest size*.**

— Antoinette *chastised* her brothers for chasing the kitten up the tree.
— When half the class arrived twenty minutes late, the teacher *chastised* them by administering a pop quiz.
— World leaders *chastised* the developing nation when it turned to nuclear armament.

chronological

kron-l-OJ-i-kuhl (*adj.*) arranged in order of time

**Though the phrase is *chronological*,
"shoot first and ask questions later" is *not logical*.**

— Suzanne's photo albums were *chronological*, except for the one fat album of travel photos.
— The police squad mapped out the events of the night in *chronological* order to better ascertain when the burglary had taken place.
— The secretary kept neat, *chronological* notes of the lengthy meeting.

DRILL 4

Refresh Your Memory

Match the word and link to its corresponding definition.

1. benign (Ben's sign)
2. berate (G-rated)
3. blandish (bland dish)
4. calumny (Cal ... glumly)
5. cajole (call Joel)
6. catalog (cattle log)
7. catalyze (cattle's eyes)
8. cavort (cave ... Ort)
9. chastise (chest size)
10. chronological (not logical)

A. to coax by using flattery
B. to scold vehemently
C. favorable, not threatening, mild
D. to leap about, behave boisterously
E. a list or collection
F. to criticize severely
G. to urge, coax
H. arranged in order of time
I. an attempt to spoil someone else's reputation by spreading lies
J. to charge, inspire

Test Your Knowledge

Fill in the blanks with the correct word from the list above. Some word forms may need changing.

1. We received a _____ from J.Crew that displayed all of their new items.

2. The local official's _____ ended up ruining his opponent's prospect of winning the election.

3. The adults ate their dinners on the patio, while the children _____ around the pool.

4. The angry boss _____ his employees for failing to meet their deadline.

5. We were all relieved to hear that the medical tests determined her tumor to be _____ .

6. Lionel carefully arranged the snapshots of his former girlfriends in _____ order, and then set fire to them.

7. Fred's buddies _____ him into attending the bachelor party.

8. After being _____ by her peers for mimicking Britney Spears, Miranda dyed her hair black and affected a Gothic style.

9. Rachel's assistant tried to _____ her into accepting the deal.

10. The president's speech _____ the nation and resuscitated the economy.

circumlocution

sur-kuhm-loh-KYOO-shun **(v.)** **indirect and wordy language**

Part of the editor's _solution_ was to cut all the _circumlocution_.

— After a bit of bumbling _circumlocution_, he finally admitted to his mistake.

— The admissions committee prefers direct language over _circumlocution_.

— Barry asked if _circumlocution_ could be a poetic device.

circumscribed

SUR-kuhm-skrahybd (*adj.*) marked off, bounded

**The *circus bride* was *circumscribed*
by clowns as circus law described.**

— Perkinsville, a tiny hamlet *circumscribed* by the Munds
  Mountains, underwent a transformation during the mining boom
  of the 1920s.
— Her social activities were greatly *circumscribed* by her father's
  unbending curfew rules.
— The rapidly deteriorating neighborhood was *circumscribed* by a
  freeway on one side and the polluted river on the other.

clandestine

klan-DES-tin *(adj.)* secret

Their spooky prophecies were *clandestine*.
Who knew the *clan's destiny* was a kick in the shin?

— David dated Mitch from Marketing but had a *clandestine* crush
on Scott from Sales.

— Hector's *clandestine* job at the CIA required him to tell his family
he worked for an international shipping company.

— Shawn considered his love of romance movies *clandestine*, but
then his wife wrote about it on her blog for everyone to see.

cloying

KLOI-ing **(*adj.*)** sickeningly sweet

The scent of the perfume was *cloying*, and her date found it extremely *annoying*.

— It was a *cloying* and overly romantic story, and Jennifer fell for it every time.

— Mrs. Sherwood wore too much perfume; if she stood by your desk in math class, it would envelop you in *cloying* cloud.

— The critics found the new dessert bar's offerings to be unsophisticated and *cloying*.

coalesce

koh-uh-LES *(v.)* to fuse into a whole

The T-shirt designer's ideas really *coalesce* when she sees Cole's really *cool "S."*

— The jury agreed that the separate testimonies all *coalesced* into a believable story.

— Three small rivers *coalesce* to form the mighty Wappern Falls.

— By the end of the night, the two small groups on either side of the dance floor had *coalesced*.

cobbler

KOB-ler (*n.*) a person who makes or repairs shoes

The Turkey Town *cobbler* created sneakers for the athletic *gobblers*.

— The *cobbler* set to work fixing the broken heels on a pair of red stilettos.

— Every spring, James brought his boots into the *cobbler* to have them resoled.

— The *cobbler's* profession is on the decline, due to the proliferation of cheap, throwaway shoes.

cogent

KOH-juhnt *(adj.)* intellectually convincing

The instructions weren't *cogent*,
so the team couldn't tell what the *coach meant*.

— Though it was a *cogent* argument, it was contextually irrelevant.

— The evidence presented was *cogent* and sound.

— Martha offered a *cogent* analysis of the mating habits of polar bears.

commensurate

kuh-MEN-ser-it (*adj.*) corresponding in size or amount

"Come, **the** *men sure ate* **all the meat, but there's a** *commensurate* **amount of dessert left for you to eat."**

— The tycoons of twentieth-century America erected mansions *commensurate* with their great wealth.

— Josephine complained that her hourly pay rate was not *commensurate* with her difficult workload.

— Since it was a self-serve buffet, everyone could get a portion of food *commensurate* to their level of hunger.

commodious

kuh-MOH-dee-uhs *(adj.)* roomy

Our hotel room seems *commodious*
until the bell boys <u>come</u> to sing an <u>ode to us</u>.

— Compared with his parents' basement, Steve's new apartment
  was bright and *commodious*.
— Brian's new winter coat was so *commodious* his little sister could
  fit inside it with him.
— Beth needed a *commodious* SUV to haul her seven children to
  soccer practice.

compensate

KOM-puhn-seyt (*adj.*) **to make an appropriate payment for something**

Dave's Diner could never *compensate* for the disgusting meal *combing Penny ate*.

— Greg was *compensated* $25 for mowing old Miss MacGregor's lawn.

— The secretary hoped his boss would *compensate* for the long hours he had put in.

— Gladys knew that a pint of ice cream wouldn't *compensate* for the breakup, but she ate it anyway.

DRILL 5

Refresh Your Memory

Match the word and link to its corresponding definition.

1. circumlocution (solution?)
2. circumscribed (circus bride)
3. clandestine (clan's destiny)
4. cloying (annoying)
5. coalesce (cool "S")
6. cobbler (gobblers)
7. cogent (coach meant)
8. commensurate (come … men sure ate)
9. commodious (come … ode to us)
10. compensate (combing Penny ate)

A. intellectually convincing
B. to make an appropriate payment for something
C. secret
D. indirect and wordy language
E. marked off, bounded
F. corresponding in size or amount
G. sickeningly sweet
H. roomy
I. to fuse into a whole
J. a person who makes or repairs shoes

Test Your Knowledge

Fill in the blanks with the correct word from the list above. Some word forms may need changing.

1. Reginald bought Sharon a new dress to _____ her for the one on which he'd spilled his ice cream.

2. I had my neighborhood _____ replace my worn-out leather soles with new ones.

3. Though Ronald was physically attractive, Maud found his constant compliments and solicitous remarks _____.

4. Holden invited the three women to join him in the backseat of the taxicab, assuring them that the car was quite _____.

5. Irene's arguments in favor of abstinence were so _____ that I could not resist them.

6. The professor's habit of speaking in _____ made it difficult to follow his lectures.

7. Gordon's ensemble of thrift-shop garments _____ into a surprisingly handsome outfit.

8. The children were permitted to play tag only within a carefully _____ area of the lawn.

9. Ahab selected a very long roll and proceeded to prepare a tuna salad sandwich _____ with his enormous appetite.

10. Announcing to her boyfriend that she was going to the gym, Sophie actually went to meet Joseph for a _____ liaison.

complicit

kuhm-PLIS-it **(adj.) being an accomplice in a wrongful act**

**She was *complicit* in the murder of Mr. Jones;
she was quite the _accomplice_ and hid all the bones.**

— Everyone present that afternoon was *complicit* in the crime that
was committed.

— The revolutionary who does not dissent is *complicit*.

— Bob watched, *complicit*, as the thieves moved a television out of
his neighbor's house.

comprehensive

com-pree-HEHN-siv (*n.*) including
everything

**The chef's *country hens sip* vitamin punch
as part of a nutritious, *comprehensive* lunch.**

— The math test was *comprehensive*, covering everything from algebra to
logarithms.
— In order to receive *comprehensive* care, the baby must see a pediatrician.
— Jamie cleaned the house *comprehensively*; she even swept behind the
refrigerator.

compunction

kuhm-PUHNGK-shuhn (*n.*) distress caused
by feeling guilty

**The poor kid felt the *compunction* to apologize
for *committing* a *punk action* that was most unwise.**

— A feeling of deep *compunction* crept over Brynn after she stole a
  tube of lipstick from the drugstore.
— Unmoved by *compunction*, Luke refused to apologize for saying
  his wife was fat.
— Alice cried tears of *compunction* and begged forgiveness from
  her sister.

conduit

KON-doo-it (*n.*) a pipe or channel through which something passes

**Reaching down the *conduit* for the diamond ring,
it was clear Connor *could do it* and get back his bling.**

— They were digging a *conduit* to allow the river to flow to the other side of town.
— The computers were connected with an elaborate system of *conduits*.
— The straw acted as a *conduit* for getting the strawberry smoothie into Greta's mouth.

congenial

kuhn-JEEN-yuhl **(adj.)** pleasantly agreeable

The twin <u>*cons, Gene and Al*</u>**, were a warden's dream:**
congenial **and never mean.**

— When Alison met her boyfriend's parents for the first time, she
was *congenial* and quiet.
— The little old lady next door seemed quite *congenial* until she
suddenly began throwing eggs at our front stoop one afternoon.
— Harold was surprised that his argumentative sister had such a
congenial daughter.

congregation

kong-gri-GEY-shuhn **(n.)** a gathering of people, especially for religious services

All the parishioners were aware of _Con Greg's station_ inside the _congregation_.

— Everyone in the *congregation* nodded solemnly as the preacher spoke.
— A *congregation* came together in the town square to hear the mysterious newcomer speak about the travels that lead him to this town.
— Before addressing the *congregation*, the rabbi cleared his throat and took two deep breaths.

consecrate

KON-si-kreyt **(v.)** to dedicate something to a holy purpose

We stopped by Father Conan's church to *consecrate* **and couldn't help but notice** *Conan's secret mate*.

— The Hindu priests traveled from India to Dallas to *consecrate* the new shrine.
— Jake was so happy to marry Gwen that their wedding kiss felt like a *consecration*.
— Klaus tried to ward off the vampire, but he forgot to get his holy water *consecrated*, so it was useless.

consolation

kon-suh-LEY-shuhn **(n.) an act of comforting**

**Con's so late**, **he missed the celebration;
they saved him a balloon—not much of a** _consolation_.

— The mother could offer no _consolation_ to her miserable child
after his ice cream cone fell on the filthy city sidewalk.
— Annie's gesture of _consolation_ was small, but meaningful: just a
squeeze of her sister's shoulder.
— Edward plowed headlong into his work, shunning any
consolation he received after being denied the promotion.

construe

kuhn-STROO (*v.*) to interpret

From the miles of traffic ahead, Mary could *construe* that there was *construction* on the *avenue*.

— He *construed* her batting eyelashes and eager smiles as an invitation for a few innocent kisses.

— Ralph didn't know how to *construe* his sister's raised eyebrows and insistent elbowing until he saw the naked guy strolling toward them on the sidewalk.

— The editor-in-chief *construed* declining ad sales as a reflection of her magazine's weak content.

consumption

kuhn-SUHMP-shuhn (*n.*) the act of consuming

**Bo's *consumption* of a *pumpkin*
made his tummy crummy and lumpy.**

— As gas prices soared, Americans wondered whether they could
  somehow reduce their gasoline *consumption*.
— Darlene thought the best way to increase her calcium
  consumption would be to eat more ice cream.
— In 2005, total meat *consumption* in the United States was about
  200 pounds per person.

DRILL 6

Refresh Your Memory

Match the word and link to its corresponding definition.

1. complicit (accomplice)
2. comprehensive (country hens sip)
3. compunction (committing … punk action)
4. conduit (could do it)
5. congenial (cons Gene and Al)
6. congregation (Con Greg's station)
7. consecrate (Conan's secret mate)
8. consolation (Con's so late)
9. construe (construction … avenue)
10. consumption (pumpkin)

A. to interpret
B. being an accomplice in a wrongful act
C. pleasantly agreeable
D. to dedicate something to a holy purpose
E. distress caused by feeling guilty
F. an act of comforting
G. including everything
H. a gathering of people, especially for religious services
I. a pipe or channel through which something passes
J. the act of consuming

Test Your Knowledge

Fill in the blanks with the correct word from the list above. Some word forms may need changing.

1. Darren found Alexandra's presence to be a _____ for his suffering.

2. The water flowed through the _____ into the container.

3. The priest told the _____ that he would be retiring.

4. _____ of intoxicating beverages is not permitted on these premises.

5. He felt _____ for the shabby way he'd treated her.

6. By keeping her daughter's affair a secret, Maddie became _____ in it.

7. His _____ manner made him popular wherever he went.

8. He _____ her throwing his clothes out the window as a signal that she wanted him to leave.

9. She sent me a _____ list of the ingredients needed to cook rabbit soufflé.

10. Arvin _____ his spare bedroom as a shrine to Christina.

convene

kuhn-VEEN (*n.*) to call together

**The gossipy nuns would weekly *convene*
to talk about the latest on the *convent scene*.**

— The bicyclists *convened* a meeting every Sunday afternoon at
  the park's North entrance.
— Before the prisoner could protest, the wardens *convened* a
  meeting to discuss his recent bad behavior.
— The boss *convened* a meeting at noon, just as his assistant was
  heading out for lunch.

convivial

con-VIV-ee-uhl **(*adj.*) characterized by feasting, drinking, merriment**

Con, Viv, and Al
are *convivial* pals.

— With more than twelve main courses, the dinner was a *convivial* affair.

— Esther's *convivial* graduation party lasted all night.

— Because Grandpa was such a jokester, his funeral was more *convivial* than somber.

convoluted

KON-vuh-loo-ted (*adj.*) intricate, complicated

The criminal's lengthy excuses were _constantly refuted_ for always being too _convoluted_.

— Mrs. Greer has a *convoluted* way of explaining algebra, but somehow the class understood her.
— Sharon's *convoluted* directions did nothing to help Taylor understand where to meet her.
— The rookie lawyer found the legal system baffling and *convoluted*.

copious

KOH-pee-uhs (*adj.*) profuse, abundant

**At the sunny beach, we biting knats were *copious*—
we delighted in how people couldn't *cope with us*.**

- The popular vegetarian potluck yielded *copious* amounts of food.
- Claire took *copious* notes as the driving instructor patiently explained how to execute a three-point turn.
- Summer in the hill towns means *copious* rainfall and long, steamy nights.

coronation

kawr-uh-NEY-shun (*v.*) the act of crowning

Queen *Cora's nation* was filled with frustration as they watched her drunk at the *coronation*.

— The little girl performed an elaborate mock *coronation*, declaring herself princess of stuffed animals.
— The *coronation* of Queen Elizabeth II took place in the summer of 1953 in front of 8,000 guests.
— The king wasted no time, ruling mercilessly from the time of his *coronation*.

corpulent

KAWR-pyuh-luhnt (*adj.*) extremely fat

**That *corpse you lent* to Dr. Jones
was so *corpulent* he couldn't find its bones.**

— Heart disease and diabetes are on the rise among the *corpulent* of the developed world.

— The monthly cigar-lover's meeting was attended by *corpulent* businessmen proud of their earnings and appetite.

— The pig won an award at the county fair because it was so *corpulent*.

coup

koo   1. (*n.*) a brilliant, unexpected act
      2. (*n.*) the overthrow of a government and assumption of authority

The chef's chickens performed a terrible *coup* when they flew right out of his *soup*.

— It was a major *coup* for Jeremy to finally beat his father at chess.
— The rebels staged a *coup* and took control of the government for twenty-four hours.
— Brianna's *coup* was to remark, after hours of silence, that she could in fact speak French.

cultivate

KUHL-tuh-veyt *(v.)* to nurture, improve, refine

The strange but caring *Cult of Eight* cultivates traits that make its members tidy and sedate.

— The new progressive elementary school believes that the arts *cultivate* the mind.

— Though he grew up in the suburbs of Chicago, Ken *cultivated* an English accent during his year abroad.

— Margaret *cultivated* several basil plants on her kitchen windowsill.

cupidity

kyoo–PID–ih–tee **(n.)** greed, strong desire

The evil genius's plan was pure *cupidity*; he'd steal all the world's water: oceans, lakes, even the *humidity*!

— The evil leader rubbed his hands together with *cupidity*, announcing that he had finally discovered where the gold was kept.

— Sociologists have agreed that *cupidity* in the middle classes has resulted in skyrocketing rates of indebtedness.

— Jack's *cupidity* was in part a product of his poor upbringing.

debase

di-BEYS *(v.)* to lower the quality or esteem of something

Janine from Brooklyn was running for *"de" base*; she ran past "de pitcha" and made him feel *debased*!

- Martha refused to *debase* her home cooking with ingredients that came from cans or jars.
- Religious leaders contend that blatant commercialism has long since *debased* the traditional meaning of Christmas.
- The restaurant's reputation was *debased* by a bad review in the local paper.

DRILL 7

Refresh Your Memory

Match the word and link to its corresponding definition.

1. convene (convent scene)
2. convivial (Con, Viv, and Al)
3. convoluted (constantly refuted)
4. copious (cope with us)
5. coronation (Cora's nation)
6. corpulent (corpse you lent)
7. coup (soup)
8. cultivate (Cult of Eight)
9. cupidity (humidity)
10. debase ("de" base)

A. greed, strong desire
B. profuse, abundant
C. to lower the quality or esteem of something
D. extreme fatness
E. to nurture, improve, refine
F. intricate, complicated
G. to call together
H. characterized by feasting, drinking, merriment
I. a brilliant, unexpected act; the overthrow of government and assumption of authority
J. the act of crowning

Test Your Knowledge

Fill in the blanks with the correct word from the list above. Some word forms may need changing.

1. At the library, she _____ her interest in spy novels.

2. The new king's _____ occurred the day after his father's death.

3. The restaurant's _____ atmosphere put me immediately at ease.

4. The large raise that he gave himself _____ his motives for running the charity.

5. Henry's _____ did not make him any less attractive to his charming, svelte wife.

6. Grace's story was so _____ that I couldn't follow it.

7. Jason _____ his entire extended family for a discussion.

8. Paul pulled off a _____ when he got a date with Cynthia by purposely getting hit by her car.

9. _____ amounts of Snapple were imbibed in the cafeteria.

10. His _____ made him enter the abandoned gold mine despite the obvious dangers.

debunk

di-BUHNGK **(v.)** to expose the falseness of something

Fiction: Plush and deep

Fact: Stiff as a board

Yes sir!

My boys **ain't soft!**

**Sergeant Al found he had to *debunk*
the rumor his soldiers slept in *deep bunks*.**

— Katie spends more time *debunking* rumors about her love life than she does enjoying it.
— The naturalist was sorry to have to *debunk* the myth of the Loch Ness monster.
— Dr. McGill *debunked* the supposed miracle drug with a host of scientific evidence.

defer

di-FUR **(v.)** to postpone something; to yield to another's wisdom

**"We can't have the wedding unless you _de-fur_,"
said Hairy Harry's fiancée, so they agreed to _defer_.**

— The weather forecast promised rain, so we had to _defer_ the picnic until next weekend.

— Joan almost always _deferred_ to her husband when it came to cooking on the grill.

— The students rejoiced when their teacher was absent and the test was _deferred_ for a week.

deft

deft **(*adj.*) skillful, capable**

The pickpocket may have been _deaf_,
but he was extremely *deft* when he made an ear theft.

— The goalie's *deft* save kept the opposing team from scoring a point.

— Gertrude worked her *deft* fingers over the embroidery before adding a tiny stitched rose.

— The car was old and rusty, but the *deft* mechanic fixed it up in a matter of minutes.

demagogue

DEM-uh-gog (*n.*) a leader who appeals to a people's prejudices

Demi's goggles let her see through political fog:
She saw which senator was the true *demagogue*.

— The *demagogue* addressed his constituents with a fiery oratory
about the threat of hell for the wicked.
— Hitler will be forever remembered as a punishing *demagogue*.
— The failing republic elected a lying *demagogue* who flooded
their nation with populist propaganda.

derelict

DER-uh-likt (*adj.*) abandoned, run-down

The cobweb-filled truck was musty and *derelict*, and Todd gasped when _Darryl licked it_.

— Catherine set out to explore the *derelict* shipyard with her digital camera in tow.

— After years of neglect and misuse, the *derelict* playground was finally torn down, and a McDonald's was built in its place.

— New York City's East Village, a vibrant neighborhood populated by artists and students, was once considered *derelict* and unsafe.

deride

dih-RIDE *(v.)* to laugh at mockingly, scorn

**The psychologist's <u>bride</u> was reduced to tears
after he *derided* her dreams and laughed at her fears.**

— The director *derided* the actor's attempt to do an English accent.
— Alana's brother *derided* her pitch, saying she threw like a girl.
— The students *deride* their substitute teacher when he mispronounces someone's name.

desecrate

DES-i-kreyt **(v.)** to violate the sacredness of a thing or place

The punks loved the wedding; they didn't *desecrate* it. Instead they found the cake and tried to *decorate* it.

— Over the weekend, the children's playground was *desecrated* with filthy graffiti and crumpled beer cans.

— Madison thought that a picnic in the cemetery sounded like fun, but her religious friend said it would be *desecration*.

— George let out a low, rumbling burp, *desecrating* the formal evening church service.

desolate

DES-uh-lit **(adj.)** deserted, dreary, lifeless

**Waiting outside a restaurant that's dark and *desolate*,
Kate begins to worry when *Des is late*.**

— Miguel's ranch was on a *desolate* 70 acres of Montana wilderness.

— Terrence kept of photograph of a *desolate* landscape in his penthouse apartment because it reminded him of the loneliness in his life that no money could replace.

— After the tornado, Dawn's neighborhood seemed *desolate* and foreign—none of the familiar landmarks remained.

destitute

DES-ti-toot *(adj.)* impoverished, utterly lacking

Des's institute **was** *destitute;*
it had no money to pay for his lab suit.

— Oblivious to real poverty, Selena complained constantly that she was *destitute* and demanded an allowance increase from her parents.

— The *destitute* old man was eventually taken in by distant relatives.

— After the hurricane, many of the struggling poor were made *destitute*.

dialect

DAHY-uh-lekt (*n.*) a variation of a language

"*Die or elect* Ted!" yelled the campaign supporters, whose strange *dialect* frightened nearby resorters.

— Gavin spoke an English *dialect* that reflected his upbringing on the mean streets of London.

— When he arrived at the remote island, he found the locals spoke a strange *dialect* of French that he could barely understand.

— The novel was translated into Spanish from a *dialect* of German.

DRILL 8

Refresh Your Memory

Match the word and link to its corresponding definition.

1. debunk (deep bunks)
2. defer (de-fur)
3. deft (deaf)
4. demagogue (Demi's goggles)
5. derelict (Darryl licked it)
6. deride (bride)
7. desecrate (decorate)
8. desolate (Des is late)
9. destitute (Des's institute)
10. dialect (die or elect)

A. skillful, capable
B. deserted, dreary, lifeless
C. impoverished, utterly lacking
D. abandoned, run-down
E. to expose the falseness of something
F. a leader who appeals to a people's prejudices
G. a variation of a language
H. to laugh at mockingly, scorn
I. to postpone something; to yield to another's wisdom
J. to violate the sacredness of a thing or place

Test Your Knowledge

Fill in the blanks with the correct word from the list above. Some word forms may need changing.

1. They feared that the construction of a golf course would _____ the preserved wilderness.

2. The _____ strengthened his hold over his people by blaming immigrants for the lack of jobs.

3. She found the _____ landscape quite a contrast to the hustle and bustle of the overcrowded city.

4. He _____ her claim to be the world's greatest chess player by defeating her in eighteen consecutive matches.

5. The bullies _____ the foreign student's accent.

6. Having worked in a bakery for many years, Marcus was a _____ bread maker.

7. Ron _____ to Diane, the expert on musical instruments, when he was asked about buying a piano.

8. The hurricane destroyed many homes and left many families _____.

9. Even though it was dangerous, the children enjoyed going to the deserted lot and playing in the _____ house.

10. In the country's remote, mountainous regions, the inhabitants spoke a _____ that the country's other inhabitants had difficulty understanding.

diaphanous

dahy-AF-uh-nuhs **(*adj.*) light, airy, transparent**

***Diane's blouse* was famous for being *diaphanous*.**

— A *diaphanous* pink curtain fluttered in the warm springtime breeze.

— The wedding dress she selected was made of layers of *diaphanous* golden tulle.

— His paintings were *diaphanous* representations of city life, with cool washes of color over meticulous drawings.

didactic

dahy-DAK-tik   **1. (*adj.*) intended to instruct**
                 2. (*adj.*) overly moralistic

**Pious Preacher Smith was constantly *didactic*—
he thought he was superior, and he sure *did act it*.**

— The *didactic* presentations of medical school were so boring as
to induce sleep.
— Irked by the lecturer's *didactic* tone, Suzanne was tempted to call
out something inflammatory.
— Many writers find it difficult to enlighten without becoming
didactic and dogmatic.

diffuse

di-FYOOZ **1. (*v.*) to scatter, thin out, break up**
di-FYOOS **2. (*adj.*) not concentrated, scattered, disorganized**

War's over, everybody! Go home!

**The weary soldiers began to *diffuse*
after the warring nations agreed to a <u>difficult truce</u>.**

— His interests were so *diffuse*, he could talk at length about almost anything.
— They intended to *diffuse* the responsibilities among five managers.
— The farmer *diffused* the cucumber seeds over a wide earthen plot.

dilatory

DIL-uh-tawr-ee *(adj.)* tending to delay, causing delay

The lonely troll's tactics are quite *dilatory*:
To cross the bridge, you'll have to *dial a story*.

— Annemarie's *dilatory* tactics gave everyone time to hide before
the birthday boy showed up for the party.

— The *dilatory* metro train system disrupted workers' schedules on
a regular basis.

— The board's *dilatory* approach meant that review of new motions
would have to wait until the next meeting.

diligent

DIL-I-juhnt **(*adj.*) showing care in doing one's work**

Dill the gent **was** *diligent*—
he never forgot to pay the rent.

— The search team was *diligent* and left no stone unturned in their quest to find the elusive stag beetle.
— Danielle was a *diligent* student and completed her homework every day immediately after school.
— The copyeditor combed through the manuscript *diligently*.

discern

di-SURN **(*v.*)** to perceive, detect

**Dave went skiing alone, but he could *discern*
a look on his friends of both *diss* and *concern*.**

— The sommelier could *discern* a mild plum flavor in the red wine
he tasted.
— Emily easily *discerned* which handbags were designer originals,
and which were cheap imitations.
— The children thought they *discerned* the shadowy shape of
a ghost moving down the dark hallway, but it was just the
family dog.

discomfit

dis-KUHM-fit **(v.)** **to thwart, baffle, make uneasy**

The groom was nervous and *discomfited* when his new tuxedo *didn't come fitted*.

— He didn't appear to be *discomfited* by the interviewer's prying questions.

— Today's science fiction features paradoxes that can *discomfit* even the most educated reader.

— The eldest child, Sam, took great pleasure in regularly *discomfiting* his younger siblings.

disgruntled

dis–GRUHN–tld **(adj.)** upset, not content

The *disgruntled* hunter hadn't seen a mammoth in days, till a _distant grunt led_ him to its hiding maze.

— A band of *disgruntled* pirates came ashore and pillaged the tiny seaside town.

— The *disgruntled* employee composed an angry email to her boss, but was too afraid to send it.

— Stephen became *disgruntled* when the dating software matched him up with homely women in distant provinces.

disheartened

dis-HAR-tend *(adj.)* feeling a loss of spirit or morale

**If sad Sam is *disheartened* once more,
his heart will *end* up flat on the floor.**

— Truman was *disheartened* by his girlfriend's lack of interest in video games.
— Patricia found the abuse of animals *disheartening* and vowed to become vegetarian.
— Rather than feel *disheartened*, the coach looked at his team's loss as learning experience.

disparage

di-SPAR-ij (*v.*) to criticize or speak ill of

The asparagus *disparaged* the carrot's *bad marriage*.

— Chuck *disparaged* the studious ways of the valedictorian, preferring to spend his afternoons smoking cigarettes under the bleachers.

— As she gained prominence, the young writer flippantly *disparaged* the work of her contemporaries.

— My mother is known to *disparage* any family member who disagrees with her way of baking apple pie.

DRILL 9

Refresh Your Memory

Match the word and link to its corresponding definition.

1. diaphanous (Diane's blouse)
2. didactic (did act it)
3. diffuse (difficult truce)
4. dilatory (dial a story)
5. diligent (Dill the gent)
6. discern (diss ... concern)
7. discomfit (didn't come fitted)
8. disgruntled (distant grunt led)
9. disheartened (his heart . . . end)
10. disparage (bad marriage)

A. showing care in doing one's work
B. upset, not content
C. to scatter, thin out, break up; not concentrated, scattered, disorganized
D. to criticize or speak ill of
E. intended to instruct; overly moralistic
F. to perceive, detect
G. tending to delay, causing delay
H. feeling a loss of spirit or morale
I. light, airy, transparent
J. to thwart, baffle, make uneasy

Test Your Knowledge

Fill in the blanks with the correct word from the list above. Some word forms may need changing.

1. The normally cheery and playful children's sudden misery _____ the teacher.

2. The child believed that his parents had unjustly grounded him, and he remained _____ for a week.

3. The general's _____ strategy enabled the enemy to regroup.

4. The saleswoman _____ the competitor's products to persuade her customers to buy what she was selling.

5. The _____ researcher made sure to check her measurements multiple times.

6. His _____ style of teaching made it seem like he wanted to persuade his students not to understand history fully, but to understand it from only one point of view.

7. He _____ the tension in the room by telling a joke.

8. The team was _____ after losing in the finals of the tournament.

9. Though he hid his emotions, she _____ from his body language that he was angry.

10. Sunlight poured in through the _____ curtains, brightening the room.

dissent

di-SENT 1. (*v.*) to disagree
2. (*n.*) the act of disagreeing

**Flower-hating Dora can get _dizzy_ from the _scents_;
she hates roses and says she really must _dissent_.**

- There was *dissent* in the family when Dad announced we wouldn't be going to Disneyland this year.
- Rachel wanted to ride the rollercoaster, but Liz *dissented*, saying it would make her sick.
- Only one of the club members *dissented* from the majority opinion.

dissonance

DIS-uh-nuhns **(*n.*)** lack of harmony or consistency

The *disco ants* said, "We can't dance to a tune that sounds like *dissonance*."

— Bradley played drums in the basement while Tricia played keyboard in her bedroom, and the resulting *dissonance* gave their father a headache.

— Polls revealed that people felt there was *dissonance* between the candidate's opinions and his behavior.

— Someone in the choir sang a bad note, and the audience could hear the *dissonance*.

dormant

DAWR-muhnt **(adj.)** sleeping, temporarily inactive

**Our _dorm ant_ knew how to party,
but now he's _dormant_ . . . that's our Marty!**

— The dog lay _dormant_ on the gleaming hardwood floors, dreaming of squirrels and meaty dinners.
— The trail maintanence project was _dormant_ until the spring thaw.
— Michelle's artistic talent remained _dormant_ until she took a painting class at the local community college.

dour

DOU-er *(adj.)* stern, joyless

Dour **Greg would always _doubt her_.**
He was so joyless, his accusations would really injure.

— Peggy's *dour* outlook on life won her few friends and even fewer lovers.

— A *dour* old librarian approached the child and scolded him for using his outdoor voice in the reading room.

— The pilot's *dour* tone over the intercom confirmed our worst fears.

eclectic

i-KLEK-tik *(adj.)* **consisting of a diverse variety of elements**

The inventor's wardrobe is really *eclectic*:
His shirt's polyester, and his pants are *electric*.

— Maya's style of dress was *eclectic*: Yesterday, she wore a men's sport coat, hot pink tights, and green high-top sneakers.
— Refusing to select just one religious belief, he sampled from many monotheistic traditions, forming his own *eclectic* spiritualism.
— Juan's term paper was well researched and drew from an *eclectic* array of sources.

effervescent

ef-er-VES-uhnt (*adj.*) bubbly, lively

**At the mall, Mark's prom date was *effervescent*—
she cheerfully helped him put *effort* into his *vest hunt*.**

— The sweet, *effervescent* beverage tickled my tongue.
— His *effervescent* mind constantly churned up new and exciting ideas.
— Mabel's *effervescent* personality quickly became irritating to her quiet roommate.

effulgent

i-FUHL-juhnt **(adj.)** radiant, splendorous

The dinner buffet was *effulgent*, and soon Sir Richard was quite *a full gent*.

— The susperstar's expensive new gold sunglasses flashed *effulgently* in the fading Miami sunlight.

— Bethany polished her pots and pans until they were as *effulgent* as a new sports car.

— Lenora's *effulgent* beauty blinded suitors to her abrasive personality.

emaciated

i-MEY-shee-ey-ted (*adj.*) **very thin, enfeebled looking**

It's odd that all the girls who *Ed Macy dated* were redheaded, frail, and *emaciated*.

— The *emaciated* old woman took small, shuffling steps toward the mailbox.
— Weighing in at barely more than eighty pounds, Lisa was *emaciated* from the cancer.
— Florence was disappointed that her daughter strove to resemble the *emaciated* models she saw in fashion magazines.

embellish

em-BEL-ish   **1. (v.) to decorate, adorn**
2. (v.) to add details to, enhance

Em's bell wished **for a prettier face,**
so it was happy when Em *embellished* **it with lace.**

— The baker *embellished* the cupcakes with delicate flowers made of pink frosting.
— Over several generations, Cinderella's fairy tale was *embellished* with various extravagant details.
— The old woman *embellishes* her simple cocktail dress with a strand of beautiful pearls.

encumber

en-KUHM-ber **(v.)** to weigh down, burden

What a bummer that the meat lovers were *encumbered* **with nothing but** *cucumbers* **for the rest of the summer.**

— The waitress felt *encumbered* by the ceaseless demands of her customers.

— Forty-pound packs *encumber* the hikers, but contain all their essential gear.

— Gina could barely get through the post office door, so *encumbered* was she with packages.

DRILL 10

Refresh Your Memory

Match the word and link to its corresponding definition.

1. dissent (dizzy ... scents)
2. dissonance (disco ants)
3. dormant (dorm ant)
4. dour (doubt her)
5. eclectic (electric)
6. effervescent (effort ... vest hunt)
7. effulgent (a full gent)
8. emaciated (Ed Macy dated)
9. embellish (Em's bell wished)
10. encumber (cucumbers)

A. to weigh down, burden
B. bubbly, lively
C. to decorate, adorn; to add details to, enhance
D. consisting of a diverse variety of elements
E. sleeping, temporarily inactive
F. radiant, splendorous
G. to disagree; the act of disagreeing
H. stern, joyless
I. lack of harmony or consistency
J. very thin, enfeebled looking

Test Your Knowledge

Fill in the blanks with the correct word from the list above. Some word forms may need changing.

1. The president's decision to increase her own salary rather than reward her employees revealed a striking _____ between her beliefs and her actions.

2. Though she pretended everything was fine, her anger lay _____ throughout the dinner party and exploded in screams of rage after everyone had left.

3. My sister eats a lot of pastries and chocolate but still looks _____.

4. My mom _____ the living room by adding lace curtains.

5. The children feared their _____ neighbor because the old man would take their toys if he believed they were being too loud.

6. At the airport, my friend was _____ by her luggage, so I offered to carry two of her bags.

7. My friend is so _____ that she makes everyone smile.

8. That bar attracts an _____ crowd: lawyers, artists, circus clowns, and investment bankers.

9. The golden palace _____ .

10. The principal argued that the child should repeat the fourth grade, but the unhappy parents _____ .

enfranchise

en-FRAN-chahyz **(v.)** to grant the vote to

**When she turned 18 and was *enfranchised*,
a dream of being mayor flashed *in Fran's eyes*.**

— Opponents of women's *enfranchisement* were often ruthless in their protests.

— The community supported the bill to *enfranchise* six-year-olds, but it never became a law.

— The Twenty-sixth Amendment to the Constitution *enfranchised* citizens over eighteen years of age.

enmity

EN-mi-tee **(n.)** ill will, hatred, hostility

**Edith ended years of *enmity*
by having tea with Hilda, her old _enemy_.**

— Sarah and Rebecca were best friends for years, but a minor
  argument suddenly resulted in *enmity* and contempt.
— After the root canal, his feelings about the dentist bordered
  on *enmity*.
— *Enmity* between the two nations resulted in a short, brutal war.

ennui

ahn-WEE (*n.*) boredom, weariness

Despite fatigue and *ennui*, <u>on we</u> strode with our really heavy load.

— "This town fills me with *ennui*," stated Mirabelle with a sigh, watching out the car window as the blank faces of apartment buildings sped by.

— The professor's two-hour lecture numbed the students with *ennui*.

— Keith was not looking forward to his wife's five-year family reunion, an event that filled him with an unbearable *ennui*.

eschew

es-CHOO *(v.)* to shun, avoid

**Picky Kenny will always *eschew*
any girl with size *E shoes*.**

— He *eschewed* his family's values when he went off to live in a
yurt in the desert.

— Carleen's new diet required that she *eschew* all grains and
starchy vegetables.

— The young protester *eschewed* violence, choosing to practice
civil disobedience instead.

esoteric

es-uh-TER-ik *(adj.)* **understood by only a select few**

The magician's book was *esoteric*; it was odd, but its contents were *especially terrific*.

— The philosophers often debated about *esoteric* topics that they nonetheless found quite engaging.

— Damien's taste in music was *esoteric*; often his girlfriend described his favorite record as being like "nails on a chalkboard."

— Professor Marden had *esoteric* interests but would occasionally comment on pop culture with his students.

exculpate

EK-skuhl-peyt **(v.)** to free from guilt or blame, exonerate

**Gerald really didn't steal his _ex's sculpted gate_;
his lawyer tried to _exculpate_ him, but he was too late.**

— The defendant was _exculpated_ when someone else involved in the trial suddenly confessed.
— She _exculpated_ herself from the charge that she was high-maintenance.
— A few sessions with his therapist allowed Benjamin to be _exculpated_ from his longstanding guilt.

exhort

ig-ZAWRT **(v.)** to urge, prod, spur

The encouraging teacher had to *exhort* her lazy students to do the book *report*.

— Whether we won or lost, the coach always *exhorted* us to do our best on the field.

— "Come on you guys," *exhorted* Septimus. "The carnival's in town for only one night!"

— Zadie tried to *exhort* her husband to walk the dog that evening after dinner; she'd already donned her pajamas.

exorbitant

ig-ZAWR-bi-tuhnt (*adj.*) excessive

The breakfast spread at the island hut was *exorbitant*: grapes, frogs' legs, *eggs, or bitter ants*.

— The neighbors found the local kids' lemonade stand prices *exorbitant* but paid them anyway.

— The *exorbitant* cost of health insurance kept Omar from seeing the doctor when he felt feverish.

— Sarah thought paying $10 for a CD was *exorbitant*, but thought nothing of a $300 iPod.

facile

FAS-il   1. (*adj.*) easy, requiring little effort
2. (*adj.*) superficial, achieved with
minimal thought or care, insincere

**The *fast eel* had a record none could beat,
but his talent was *facile* and no huge feat.**

— The soccer team achieved a *facile* victory over its longstanding
rivals.

— Maria found her term paper to be *facile* and offered to write her
best friend's paper, too.

— Their understanding of nuclear physics was *facile*, but they
listened anyway as the professor described his research.

fatuous

FAT-you-uhs *(adj.)* silly, foolish

The **Fat U.S.** flag should have a cheeseburger on it, and vertical stripes for a "slimming" effect...

Kim looked serious but was *fatuous* when she said America should be "*Fat U.S.*"

— Lucy's belief in fairies was *fatuous*, but persisted long into her twenties.
— The child's constant, *fatuous* questions irritated the babysitter.
— The old man was always hollering *fatuously* for kids to keep the noise down outside his apartment.

DRILL 11

Refresh Your Memory

Match the word and link to its corresponding definition.

1. enfranchise (in Fran's eyes)
2. enmity (enemy)
3. ennui (on we)
4. eschew (E shoes)
5. esoteric (especially terrific)
6. exculpate (ex's sculpted gate)
7. exhort (report)
8. exorbitant (eggs, or bitter ants)
9. facile (fast eel)
10. fatuous (victorious)

A. excessive
B. boredom, weariness
C. ill will, hatred, hostility
D. understood by only a select few
E. easy, requiring little effort
F. to shun, avoid
G. to grant the vote to
H. to urge, prod, spur
I. to free from guilt or blame, exonerate
J. silly, foolish

Test Your Knowledge

Fill in the blanks with the correct word from the list above. Some word forms may need changing.

1. This game is so _____ that even a four-year-old can master it.

2. Henry _____ his colleagues to join him in protesting against the university's hiring policies.

3. George hates the color green so much that he _____ all green food.

4. Her _____ praise made me blush and squirm in my seat.

5. Even the most advanced students cannot understand the physicist's _____ theories.

6. I feel such _____ that I don't look forward to anything, not even my birthday party.

7. Mark and Andy have clearly not forgiven each other, because the _____ between them is obvious to anyone in their presence.

8. My discovery of the ring behind the dresser _____ me from the charge of having stolen it.

9. The Nineteenth Amendment _____ women.

10. He considers himself a serious poet, but in truth, he only writes _____ limericks.

fecund

FEK-uhnd (*adj.*) fruitful, fertile

**Though Sarah's soil was *fecund*,
her peaches only placed *second*.**

— As they age, people lose the active and *fecund* imagination of childhood.
— The *fecund* garden produced a bumper crop of zucchini for the third year in a row.
— The hikers were amazed at how lush and *fecund* the forest was.

feral

FER-uhl **(adj.)** wild, savage

Flo found a *feral* <u>ferret</u>, and when she brought it home, no one could train it.

— A group of *feral* dogs chased Rama six blocks before they were distracted by a neighborhood cat.

— During her pregnancy, Rosemary had a consuming, almost *feral* appetite for rare meat.

— He had always been interested in the myth of the *feral* boy raised by a pack of wolves.

flagrant

FLEY-gruhnt (*adj.*) offensive, egregious

To use a public fountain as a bathtub is *flagrant*, but where else can you wash your hair as a <u>vagrant</u>?

— The local government was known for its *flagrant* disregard of the very law it established.

— When she got back the test, Erin couldn't believe the number of *flagrant* errors she'd made.

— Tony took off his clothes and jumped in the park fountain, committing a *flagrant* act of public nudity.

florid

FLOR-id **(*adj.*) flowery, ornate**

The dress Flora bought was unusually *florid*, and we were quite _floored_ by it.

— Hilary detested the *florid* wallpaper in her grandmother's kitchen.

— The bridesmaids wore orange dresses printed with a *florid* pattern.

— For his thirtieth birthday, Clark received a card with a *florid* inscription from his great-aunt Edna.

forbearance

fawr–BAIR–uhns (*n.*) patience, restraint, toleration

Four bear aunts **ran for the honey plants because they lacked** *forbearance*.

— Linda showed great *forbearance* in her treatment of the fidgety toddler.

— He felt that truth, compassion, and *forbearance* were the greatest virtues and strove to achieve them in his everyday life.

— The elderly man lacked *forbearance* and was given to yelling at anyone who got in his way at the grocery store.

forlorn

fawr-LAWRN (*adj.*) lonely, abandoned, hopeless

Lonely Joe was very *forlorn*.
No one could get to his house with _four lawns_.

— The *forlorn* child wandered around the fringes of the abandoned playground.
— Tricia adopted three of the *forlorn* kittens she saw at the local animal shelter.
— The old man sat at the corner table every evening at five o'clock, looking more *forlorn* and miserable every day.

frivolous

FRIV-uh-luhs **(adj.)** of little importance, trifling

**Liv thought primping was *frivolous*,
but with her *frizzy* hair, she could do no *less*.**

— The judge felt that the lawyer's concerns were *frivolous* and dismissed his objections.
— Karen knew that collecting antique salt-and-pepper shakers was a *frivolous* pursuit, but she enjoyed it nonetheless.
— Pete finally spoke up during the town meeting, but his suggestion was deemed *frivolous* and unnecessary.

furtive

FUR-tiv *(adj.)* secretive, sly

The werewolf is *furtive* and sneaky at night because his <u>fur</u> grows great lengths when the moon is bright.

— Dana exchanged a *furtive* glance with her cute coworker during the company meeting.

— He had a *furtive* manner better suited to a burglar or used-car salesman.

— Brandon finally admitted to having taken a few *furtive* looks at his sister's diary.

garrulous

GEHR-you-lus **(adj.)** talkative, wordy

Gary **and** *Lou* **were a** *garrulous* **two;**
they talked so much, their faces turned blue.

— The *garrulous* salesman tried to convince Laura to buy the car.

— The mayor had a *garrulous* manner that irritated his constituents.

— Leslie's *garrulous* little brother kept her from getting to the prom on time.

gratuitous

gruh-TOO-i-tuhs **(adj.)** uncalled for, **unwarranted**

Our fairy godmother has been really <u>great to us</u>, **but the glass slippers and gilded carriage are a little** *gratuitous*.

— The critic was annoyed by the *gratuitous* violence in an otherwise entertaining film.

— Amy heaped *gratuitous* praise upon her boss, hoping for a promotion.

— Annoyed, Justin spat out a *gratuitous* insult at the customer service representative on the other side of the desk.

DRILL 12

Refresh Your Memory

Match the word and link to its corresponding definition.

1. fecund (second)
2. feral (ferret)
3. flagrant (vagrant)
4. florid (floored)
5. forbearance (four bear aunts)
6. forlorn (four lawns)
7. frivolous (frizzy ... less)
8. furtive (fur)
9. garrulous (Gary ... Lou)
10. gratuitous (great to us)

A. lonely, abandoned, hopeless
B. secretive, sly
C. uncalled for, unwarranted
D. fruitful, fertile
E. flowery, ornate
F. wild, savage
G. offensive, egregious
H. of little importance, trifling
I. patience, restraint, toleration
J. talkative, wordy

Test Your Knowledge

Fill in the blanks with the correct word from the list above. Some word forms may need changing.

1. Even though I had the flu, my family decided to go skiing for the weekend and leave me home alone, feeling feverish and _____ .

2. The judge's decision to set the man free simply because the man was his brother was a _____ abuse of power.

3. That beast looks so _____ that I would fear being alone with it.

4. Some day, all that anxiety about whether your zit will disappear before the prom will seem totally _____ .

5. The writer's _____ prose belongs on a sentimental Hallmark card.

6. Some talk show hosts are so _____ that their guests can't get a word in edgewise.

7. Jane's placement of her drugs in her sock drawer was not as _____ as she thought, as the sock drawer is the first place most parents look.

8. The _____ tree bore enough apples to last us the entire season.

9. The doctor showed great _____ in calming down the angry patient who shouted insults at him.

10. Every morning, the guy at the doughnut shop gives me a _____ helping of ketchup packets.

gregarious

gri-GAIR-ee-uhs **(adj.)** drawn to the company of others, sociable

**Normally shy _Greg_ became _gregarious_,
flirting with girls and telling jokes that were _hilarious_.**

— Carol's _gregarious_ nature meant she hated her job as a lighthouse keeper.
— The _gregarious_ puppy would greet any stranger on the street with a wet, sloppy kisses.
— Jared wasn't very atheletic but played baseball because he was _gregarious_ and wanted to be part of a team.

gourmand

goor-MAHND **(n.) someone fond of eating and drinking**

The world's top *gourmand*
cooked eighty patties to be crowned *Gourmet Man*.

— Amy secured her reputation as a *gourmand* after hosting several
lavish dinner parties for her friends.
— Though he could stand to lose a few pounds, Jean-Michel was
an unabashed *gourmand*.
— Robert fancied himself a *gourmand*, but he detested cheeses of
all kinds and refused to eat anything containing onions.

harrowing

HAR-oh-ing *(adj.)* greatly distressing, vexing

**Sophie found the fun house *harrowing*;
she screamed when the walls seemed to be *narrowing*.**

— The film was a *harrowing* look at the impact of racism on a
London suburb in the 1950s.

— The young woman described her week stranded in the woods as
a *harrowing* and unforgettable experience.

— The Chronicle of Higher Education produced a *harrowing* report
on the prevalence of eating disorders in female collegiate
athletes.

haughty

HAW-tee (*adj.*) disdainfully proud

The billionaire's daughter was a _hottie_, but she was snotty and _haughty_.

— The *haughty* old woman dined only at the finest establishments, even as her savings dwindled and her health deteriorated.

— When I mentioned stopping by the dollar store after work, my friend gave me a *haughty* look and said she had other plans.

— The salesclerk at the perfume counter was unusually *haughty*, and sneered openly at her customers.

hegemony, hand gems for money

hegemony

heh-JEM-uh-nee **(n.)** domination over others

The diamond company's *hegemony* kept others from selling <u>gems for money</u>.

— The Marxist philosopher Antonio Gramsci wrote extensively on the topic of cultural *hegemony*.

— Conflict over *hegemony* has been at the root of wars throughout history.

— To counter American *hegemony*, China has formed alliances with Russia and Central Asia.

hiatus

hahy-EY-tuhs **(n.)** **a break or gap in duration or continuity**

We thought the evil giant had taken an eating *hiatus*, but then *he ate us*.

— After two seasons of disappointing ratings, June's favorite TV show went on permanent *hiatus*.

— Mary Ellen's advice column had a six-week *hiatus* when she gave birth to her first child.

— Debbie didn't think of it as a breakup, but as a "relationship *hiatus*."

hypothetical

hahy-puh-THET-i-kuhl (*adj.*) supposed or assumed true, but unproven

The *hippo* acted *theoretical* when he was *hypothetical* about why the medical book was alphabetical.

— Doctor Quackenbush's theory was *hypothetical* for now, but he hoped to test it once he was finished building the time machine.

— When his girlfriend stayed out late, Ross imagined *hypothetical* situations involving her and her other lovers.

— The preacher's ideas were *hypothetical*, at best, but his believers ardently defended him.

illicit

i-LIS-it **(*adj.*) forbidden, not permitted**

It's *illicit* to get drunk and feel *ill in this city*.
Plus, you're sloppy, and that isn't pretty.

— As a child, Rebecca kept an *illicit* stash of gummy bears under
  her bed.
— The squatters were arrested for the possession of *illicit* drugs.
— He had *illicit* motives for reducing his business taxes.

impeccable

im-PEK-uh-buhl (*adj.*) exemplary, flawless

The kids' ice fort was *impeccable*, snowball-resistant and <u>unwreckable</u>.

— Melanie arrived at work that morning looking *impeccable*, but by the end of the day, her hair was wild and her skirt was stained with ink.

— Martin had an *impeccable* attendance record so he received the perfect attendance award at the end of the year.

— Because of her *impeccable* handwriting, Julia was often asked to address envelopes.

impecunious

im-pi-KYOO-nee-uhs *(adj.)* poor

The *impecunious* nephew could not pay his rent,
so his *impish* and *peculiar* uncle set up a tent.

— Dorothy often sent care packages of cookies or warm sweaters to her *impecunious* young artist friend.

— In those days, he was *impecunious* but happy, living in a tiny apartment with a window overlooking a dark alley.

— The family was *impecunious*, but with the help of their church, they managed to have a warm and filling Christmas dinner.

DRILL 13

Refresh Your Memory

Match the word and link to its corresponding definition.

1. gregarious (Greg … hilarious)
2. gourmand (Gourmet Man)
3. harrowing (narrowing)
4. haughty (hottie)
5. hegemony (gems for money)
6. hiatus (he ate us)
7. hypothetical (hippo … theoretical)
8. illicit (ill in this city)
9. impeccable (unwreckable)
10. impecunious (impish … peculiar)

A. drawn to the company of others, sociable
B. greatly distressing, vexing
C. domination over others
D. supposed or assumed true, but unproven
E. poor
F. disdainfully proud
G. someone fond of eating and drinking
H. forbidden, not permitted
I. exemplary, flawless
J. a break or gap in duration or continuity

Test Your Knowledge

Fill in the blanks with the correct word from the list above. Some word forms may need changing.

1. Even though it has been celebrated by seven major newspapers, that the drug will be a success when tested in humans is still _____ .

2. The _____ in service should last two or three months—until the cable lines are repaired.

3. My parents, who used to eat little more than crackers and salad, have become real _____ in their old age.

4. The car crash was a _____ experience, but I have a feeling that the increase in my insurance premiums will be even more upsetting.

5. The fourth-grader learned many _____ words from a pamphlet that was being passed around school.

6. "I fear he's too _____ to take me out tonight," the bratty girl whined.

7. The superstar's _____ dismissal of her costars will backfire on her someday.

8. Britain's _____ over its colonies was threatened once nationalist sentiment began to spread around the world.

9. Well, if you're not _____ , I don't know why you would want to go to a singles party!

10. If your grades were as _____ as your sister's, then you too would receive a car for a graduation present.

implicit

im-PLIS-it *(adj.)* understood but not outwardly obvious, implied

It goes without saying, it's rather *implicit*, the end of a rainbow is where an *imp will sit*.

— Brenda and Sam agreed that the *implicit* sign that they wanted to leave the party would be a scratch on the side of the nose.

— The chairman of the board felt that the shareholders expressed an *implicit* criticism of his practices in their latest report.

— They had an *implicit* agreement to skip class together on Wednesday, but never spoke about it aloud for fear of being overheard by their teacher.

inane

i-NAYN *(adj.)* silly, foolish

Having one state lobster is OK *in Maine*,
but two state lobsters is just *inane*.

— The scientist was increasingly irritated at the barrage of *inane* questions issued by the students.

— Danielle could barely stand to engage in the kind of *inane* conversation required in the workplace and kept her headphones on for most of the day.

— Their romance was an *inane* summer fling; come September, they'd both forget about it altogether.

inarticulate

in-ahr-TIK-yuh-lit (*adj.*) incapable of expressing oneself clearly through speech

The terrible reporter is *inarticulate*—
plus his spelling's bad and his <u>*article's late*</u>.

— Nora's *inarticulate* boyfriend made her mixtapes instead of telling her how much he loved her.
— Though the president was clumsy and *inarticulate*, the nation trusted him to lead them into war.
— Barry considered his *inarticulate* drunken rambling to be poetry, and tried to charge passersby a dollar to listen to him shout.

incisive

in-SAHY-siv *(adj.)* clear, sharp, direct

Indecisive **Marty was not *incisive* when he called, so Becky didn't know if he was going to come at all.**

— The store manager explained, in an *incisive* tone of voice, that shoplifting was absolutely not allowed.
— Jenny summarized the entire lecture with three *incisive* bullet points.
— The child had an *incisive* mind for mathematics, and stunned his teachers by rapidly solving complex equations.

incontrovertible

in-kon-truh-VUR-tuh-buhl (*adj.*) indisputable

The proof is *incontrovertible*:
Girls love guys with *convertibles*.

— The lawyer submitted the document as *incontrovertible* proof of his client's innocence.

— Luke thought his logic was *incontrovertible*, but he was defeated at the state debate championship.

— Though Darwin's theory of evolution is *incontrovertible*, religious zealots continue to debate its veracity.

incorrigible

in-KOR-i-juh-buhl **(adj.)** incapable of correction, delinquent

The ranch's new cowboy is *incorrigible*; they just can't make him *encourage a bull*.

— Zeke's *incorrigible* nail-biting habit lasted well through adulthood.

— As punishment for talking back to her mother, the *incorrigible* child was sent to her room for the rest of the night.

— Cara was an *incorrigible* liar—she fibbed to her husband about even the most mundane things.

indigenous

in-DIJ-uh-nuhs (*adj.*) originating in a region

The botanist found local plants that were *indigenous* when he came on the dinosaur *dig with us*.

— The saguaro cactus is *indigenous* to the Sonoran Desert of southern Arizona and northern Mexico.

— The *indigenous* peoples of western Alaska demanded recognition for their fishing prowess.

— Caribbean cooking is dependent on both the flavors of *indigenous* plants and animals and on European and African influences.

indigent

IN-di-juhnt *(adj.)* very poor, impoverished

Though he was half-starved and obviously *indigent*, when I offered money to Uncle Mort, he became rather *indignant*.

— The charitable organization prided itself in providing food relief for the *indigent* populations of northwestern Smithfield county.

— Blake's conservative opinions about welfare and the *indigent* caused him to get into arguments with his more liberal friends.

— Tired of nature-channel specials on *indigent* people in barren landscapes, Moira changed the channel to watch the latest reality show.

indignation

in-dig-NEY-shuhn **(n.)** **anger sparked by something unjust or unfair**

In Dig Nation **there's** *indignation*
about cancelling the shoveling celebration.

— The rejection letter from Justin's top choice college filled him with *indignation*.

— The protesters showed their *indignation* by shouting and carrying signs bearing antiwar slogans.

— Rachel was careful not to let her *indignation* show after her boss called her a hothead during the company meeting.

indomitable

in-DOM-i-tuh-buhl **(adj.) not capable of being conquered**

The pitcher was *indomitable*, each hard pitch landing *in Dom's mitt*.

— An *indomitable* lion guards the castle door.
— History will soon prove that the American army is no longer an *indomitable* force.
— The *indomitable* bear survived, even after being pummeled by the hunter's arrows.

DRILL 14

Refresh Your Memory

Match the word and link to its corresponding definition.

1. implicit (imp will sit)
2. inane (in Maine)
3. inarticulate (article's late)
4. incisive (indecisive)
5. incontrovertible (convertibles)
6. incorrigible (encourage a bull)
7. indigenous (dig with us)
8. indigent (indignant)
9. indignation (in Dig Nation)
10. indomitable (in Dom's mitt)

A. clear, sharp, direct
B. understood but not outwardly obvious, implied
C. originating in a region
D. anger sparked by something unjust or unfair
E. incapable of correction, delinquent
F. incapable of expressing oneself clearly through speech
G. silly, foolish
H. very poor, impoverished
I. indisputable
J. not capable of being conquered

Test Your Knowledge 14

Fill in the blanks with the correct word from the list above. Some word forms may need changing.

1. You can buy Grandma nicotine gum all you want, but I think that after sixty-five years of smoking, she's _____ .

2. The discussion wasn't going anywhere until her _____ comment allowed everyone to see what the true issues were.

3. I know Professor Smith didn't actually say not to write from personal experience, but I think such a message was _____ in her instruction to use scholarly sources.

4. Though he spoke for more than an hour, the lecturer was completely _____ and the students had no idea what he was talking about.

5. To be honest, Jim, my _____ nature means I could never take orders from anyone, and especially not from a jerk like you.

6. I would rather donate money to help the _____ population than to the park sculpture fund.

7. Some fear that these plants, which are not _____ to the region, may choke out the vegetation that is native to the area.

8. Only stubborn Tina would attempt to disprove the _____ laws of physics.

9. Some films are so _____ that the psychology of the characters makes absolutely no sense.

10. I resigned from the sorority because of my _____ at its hazing of new members.

inextricable

in-ik-STRIK-uh-buhl (*adj.*) hopelessly tangled or entangled

**Numbskull Nathan was very _trickable_;
he got himself into a situation that was _inextricable_.**

— The chewing gum was lodged *inextricably* in the little girl's hair.
— In a dusty corner of the office, the power cords lay in an
  inextricable pile.
— Tammy's lies resulted in a maze of *inextricable* excuses.

infamy

IN-fuh-mee **(adj.)** notoriety, extreme ill repute

The Barkleys had a reputation of *infamy*; their penchant for stealing neighbors' underwear was *in the family*.

— Due to his bumbling of foreign policy, the president was sure to be remembered in *infamy*.

— For an entire generation, December 7, 1941 will be remembered as a day of *infamy*.

— Cletus regarded his history of incarceration as a badge of *infamy*.

ingenuous

in-JEN-you-uhs **(adj.)** not devious; innocent
and candid

In Jen you trust—she's *ingenuous*—
you know she'd never lie to us.

— Maria found it refreshing to work with children because of their
ingenuous manner.
— Though she had prepared something comedic and cynical,
Chelsea instead gave an *ingenuous*, heartfelt speech about her
best friend, the bride.
— He asked *ingenuously* if the two of them were dating, and they
both stammered out a negative reply.

iniquity

i-NIK-wi-tee (*n.*) wickedness or sin

Crime doesn't pay *in Nick's city*—
in his town there are laws against all *iniquity*.

— The thieves reveled in their *iniquity*, lounging carelessly on shabby furnishings while watching cable on their purloined thirty-six-inch television.

— Harold and his brother regularly practiced small acts of *iniquity*, such as salting slugs and pulling the legs off spiders.

— The drug dealer and his young girlfriend lived not in *iniquity*, but in a large mansion in the nice part of town.

innocuous

i-NOK-yoo-uhs (*adj.*) harmless, inoffensive

**Sticks and stones can <u>knock you unconscious</u>,
but words, as they say, are rather *innocuous*.**

— Laura assured her daughter that broccoli was *innocuous*, but
little Leslie refused to even nibble a piece.
— Our boss exploded with rage after the senior manager made
what everyone thought was a perfectly *innocuous* remark.
— Most spiders are *innocuous*, and can actually help keep your
home free of other insects.

innuendo

in-yoo-EN-doh (*adj.*) an insinuation

**The *innuendo* reached a *crescendo*
when Dan suggested Sam took his friend's dough.**

— The local paper was filled with *innuendo*, half-truths, and
outright lies about the incumbent mayor.

— Mike picked up easily on Sarah's suggestive *innuendo*.

— Not one for *innuendo*, Liz preferred to be forthright when
gossiping about her coworkers.

insinuate

in–SIN–yoo–eyt **(v.)** to suggest indirectly or subtly

"I believe you're _in sin_ with what _you ate_. Do you really think it's kosher?" he _insinuates_.

— The doctor _insinuated_ with raised eyebrows that he didn't approve of his patient's diet of bacon and eggs.

— Janet turned, cried out angrily to the student behind her, "Are you _insinuating_ that I cheated on the test?"

— The detective _insinuated_ that the two suspects were lying.

insipid

in-SIP-id (*adj.*) dull, boring

Though the drink was tasteless and *insipid*, Peter dutifully *in-sipped it*.

— The restaurant had gotten good reviews, but Pauline thought the dinner she had there was *insipid*.

— This year's crop of art students excelled at cranking out *insipid*, thoughtless work.

— Todd ended the date early after growing irritated at his girlfriend's *insipid* attempts at conversation.

insular

INS-yuh-ler **(adj.)** separated and narrow-minded; tight-knit, closed off

Insular **Hector lives off the grid**
in a solar **house with his wife and kid.**

— The novelist lead an *insular* and private life; he rejected all interview requests and rarely made public appearances.

— Residents of the farming community had *insular* views about foreigners.

— Ines hadn't realized the women's college would be so cliquey and *insular*; she struggled to find a group with which she felt comfortable.

intransigent

in-TRAN-si-juhnt **(adj.)** refusing to compromise, often on an extreme opinion

The beautiful young girl was *intransigent*:
She refused to believe her looks could *entrance a gent*.

— The king remained *intransigent*, even while his country was bombed and the treaty revoked.

— Charles was sometimes *intransigent*, sometimes relaxed and easygoing.

— The union was *intransigent* in its opposition to a longer workweek.

DRILL 15

Refresh Your Memory

Match the word and link to its corresponding definition.

1. inextricable (trickable)
2. infamy (in the family)
3. ingenuous (in Jen you trust)
4. iniquity (in Nick's city)
5. innocuous (knock you unconscious)
6. innuendo (crescendo)
7. insinuate (in sin ... you ate)
8. insipid (in-sipped it)
9. insular (in a solar)
10. intransigent (entrance a gent)

A. separated and narrow-minded; tight-knit, closed off
B. not devious; innocent and candid
C. dull, boring
D. an insinuation
E. refusing to compromise, often on an extreme opinion
F. notoriety, extreme ill repute
G. harmless, inoffensive
H. to suggest indirectly or subtly
I. hopelessly tangled or entangled
J. wickedness or sin

Test Your Knowledge

Fill in the blanks with the correct word from the list above. Some word forms may need changing.

1. The play was so _____ , I fell asleep halfway through.

2. He must have writers, but his speeches seem so _____, it's hard to believe he's not speaking from his own heart.

3. I wish Luke and Spencer would stop _____ that my perfect report card is the result of anything other than my superior intelligence and good work habits.

4. Because of the sensitive nature of their jobs, those who work for the CIA must remain _____ and generally only discuss work matters with one another.

5. "Your _____ ," said the priest to the practical jokester, "will be forgiven."

6. Unless I look at the solution manual, I have no way of solving this _____ problem.

7. During the debate, the politician made several _____ about the sexual activities of his opponent.

8. The _____ of his crime will not lessen as the decades pass.

9. In spite of their _____ appearance, these mushrooms are actually quite poisonous.

10. The _____ child said he would have twelve scoops of ice cream, or he would bang his head against the wall until his mother fainted from fear.

inundate

IN-uhn-deyt (*v.*) to flood with abundance

Cuddly Sam will *inundate* you with kisses, but *on a date*, he may scare his little missus.

— After the pretty cheerleader put out a call for help on her term paper, she was *inundated* with volunteer tutors.

— The city streets were *inundated* with foul water after the sewer system sprang a major leak.

— Margaret planted too much zucchini in her garden and was *inundated* with the vegetable come August.

irreverence

i-REV-er-uhns **(n.)** disrespect

In the middle of the sermon, with great *irreverence*, Irma stuck her tongue out at the <u>reverends</u>.

— Jolene treated her managers at work with *irreverence*, and she was promoted, much to the surprise of her coworkers.

— Though Delbert was mayor of his small town, his children were *irreverent*, and called him "bonehead."

— The young punks cultivated an attitude of *irreverence* and regarded their parents' values with sneering disapproval.

judicious

joo-DISH-uhs *(adj.)* **having or exercising sound judgment**

**It isn't very *judicious*
to juggle with *Jud's dishes*.**

— Stephanie depended on the words of wisdom doled out by her *judicious* older sister.
— The police officer took a *judicious* pause before issuing the traffic ticket.
— The chef was *judicious* in his use of hot pepper flakes.

languid

LANG-gwid (*adj.*) sluggish from fatigue
or weakness

**The *languid squid*
relaxes with his kid.**

— The illness had turned Sophia from an energetic young athlete to
  a tired and *languid* convalescent.
— Normally, he wouldn't be tired, but the wet heat of a midsummer
  afternoon in Georgia made him exhausted and *languid*.
— Pushed to his limit by the sprints he had run before the game,
  the shortstop mopped sweat from his brow and walked *languidly*
  to third base.

largess

lahr-JES **(n.)** the generous giving
of lavish gifts

The *large S* was known for his *largess*:
He gave gifts to all the rest.

— The millionaire dispensed of his money with uncharacteristic
largess.

— Morgan was astonished at her grandmother's *largess* during
Christmastime and promptly began to write a thank-you note.

— The recipients of the organization's *largess* were mostly
impoverished families in the Cambridge area.

laudatory

LAW-di-tor-ee **(*adj.*)** expressing
admiration or praise

Laurie's laudatory story
got all the glory.

— The valedictorian received a *laudatory* citation.
— His mother's *laudatory* speech embarrassed Dave.
— Debbie made a *laudatory* comment to the lead singer of her
favorite band.

lavish

LAV-ish **1. (*adj.*) given without limits**
2. (*v.*) to give without limits

**Aunt Trish was *lavish* but somewhat *late-ish*;
every hour she missed earned Pete a new goldfish.**

— Only the most wealthy subjects of the kingdom were invited to the prince's *lavish* banquet.
— Craig's friends criticized him for *lavishing* his girlfriend with expensive jewelry and perfumes.
— The artist was skeptical of anyone who issued *lavish* praise of her work.

legerdemain

lej-er-duh-MEYN (*n.*) deception, slight-of-hand

The Garden Man has got a crooked brain;
He steals houseplants with _legerdemain_.

— Known for his _legerdemain_, the card shark was eventually kicked out of the casino.
— The magician relied on _legerdemain_ to perform his conjuring feats for the audience.
— Using a bit of _legerdemain_, Jill explained to the customs official that the fruit was fake, and was to be used in a photo shoot.

magnanimous

mag-NAN-uh-muhs *(adj.)* noble, generous

Megan the mouse **was** *magnanimous*;
she shared her house with all of us.

— The king was a wise and *magnanimous* ruler.
— Too *magnanimous* to resent his friend for getting into Harvard, Derrick instead vowed to make the best of his four years at Yale.
— Though stern and uncompromising with his business associates, the businessman's dealings with charities were *magnanimous*.

malevolent

muh-LEV-uh-luhnt **(*adj.*) wanting harm to befall others**

He looks like a killer!

Our new hamster is vicious and *malevolent*; one look at him, and it's clear that _male is violent_.

— Recently, American citizens began to feel *malevolent* toward their president because of his brash foreign policy.

— His insecurities made Arthur *malevolent* toward more successful artists.

— The *malevolent* witch gave a sleeping potion to her prisoner so she couldn't escape.

DRILL 16

Refresh Your Memory

Match the word and link to its corresponding definition.

1. inundate (on a date)
2. irreverence (reverends)
3. judicious (Jud's dishes)
4. languid (squid)
5. largess (large S)
6. laudatory (Laurie's story)
7. lavish (late-ish)
8. legerdemain (The Garden Man)
9. magnanimous (Megan the mouse)
10. malevolent (male is violent)

A. disrespect
B. noble, generous
C. to flood with abundance
D. the generous giving of lavish gifts
E. wanting harm to befall others
F. given without limits
G. having or exercising sound judgment
H. sluggish from fatigue or weakness
I. deception, slight-of-hand
J. expressing admiration or praise

Test Your Knowledge

Fill in the blanks with the correct word from the list above. Some word forms may need changing.

1. Although I had already broken most of her dishes, Jacqueline was _____ enough to continue letting me use them.

2. Such _____ comments are unusual from someone who is usually so reserved in his opinions.

3. In the summer months, the great heat makes people _____ and lazy.

4. The _____ displayed by the band that marched through the chapel disturbed many churchgoers.

5. Because I am the star of a new sitcom, my fans are sure to _____ me with fan mail and praise.

6. My boss demonstrated great _____ by giving me a new car.

7. The _____ old man sat in the park all day, tripping unsuspecting passersby with his cane.

8. Because they had worked very hard, the performers appreciated the critic's _____ praise.

9. When the _____ king decided to compromise rather than send his army to its certain death, he was applauded.

10. Smuggling the French plants through customs by claiming that they were fake was a remarkable bit of _____ .

179

malleable

MAL-ee-uh-buhl **(*adj.*) capable of being shaped or transformed**

**Joe says anything's *malleable*
if you hit and are *mallet-able*.**

— Caitlin's *malleable* personality was responsible for her obsession with every passing fad.
— In his practiced hands, the *malleable* clay soon became a beautiful vase.
— Though it is a *malleable* metal, silver is also strong and nearly indestructible.

manifest

MAN-uh-fest **1. (*adj.*) easily understandable, obvious**
2. (*v.*) to show plainly

The requirements are *manifest*:
only manly men at the _Manly Fest_.

— The local government's corruption was made *manifest* after the mayor appointed his brother to the city council.
— Signs of skin cancer often *manifest* long after the original sun damage is done.
— The mother's happiness was *manifest* as the baby crawled slowly toward her.

manifold

MAN-uh-fohld (*adj.*) diverse, varied

"Come on, *man, fold* it! Finish your *manifold* chores!
We're here to skate, not to watch you do more!"

— As executive chef, one of his *manifold* duties was to inspect every dish before it went out to the dining room.
— The group's appeal was *manifold*: They produced accessible, poppy music, with smart lyrics and a danceable beat.
— There were *manifold* reasons for the company's failure, not one simple cause.

maudlin

mawd-lin *(adj.)* weakly sentimental

**Here is *maudlin Maude in* her blankie,
cuddlin' and kissin' his hankie.**

— His girlfriend cried throughout the movie's ending, but Billy
  found it to be *maudlin*.
— After a few drinks, Martha began telling *maudlin* stories about
  the stuffed animals she had loved in childhood.
— The slideshow was supposed to honor the history of the college,
  but it turned *maudlin* after the president inserted several slides
  of her old dog.

mawkish

MAW-kish **(adj.) characterized by sick sentimentality**

Ma kissed her grown son,
saying *mawkishly*, "You're still my sweet little one."

— A *mawkish* ending undermined the entire movie.
— Scott was moved by the tribute, but his brother found it *mawkish*.
— Though the writer was often criticized for having an irrepressible *mawkish* streak, his books were revered by millions.

maxim

MAK-sim **(n.)** a common saying expressing a principle of conduct

"Just be yourself" was ugly Charlie's *maxim*.
But his face is so scary we've chosen to <u>*mask him*</u>.

— Gwen was a firm believer in the *maxim* that one must learn the rules before breaking them.
— Disgusted by the president's moralistic *maxims*, the senator wrote a long and damning editorial for the Sunday paper.
— Even at age ninety, Mae was able to easily repeat the simple *maxims* she had been taught in elementary school.

metamorphosis

met-uh-MAWR-fuh-sis **(*adj.*) the change of
form, shape, substance**

**Jane's magic pill made her <u>*morph a full size*</u> smaller,
and the *metamorphosis* made her friend seem taller.**

— Everyone was surprised at Katie's *metamorphosis* from shy math
geek to angry punk rocker the summer after junior year.
— After twelve weeks of weightlifting, Mike's body went through a
muscular *metamorphosis*.
— The American lifestyle underwent a radical *metamorphosis* to
adapt to the conditions of life during World War II.

mitigate

MIT-i-geyt **(v.)** to make less violent, alleviate

It's hard to *mitigate* the sadness of the softball players; with their *mitts in a gate*, their days are much grayer.

— The only thing that could *mitigate* Chester's grounding was the stash of candy bars he kept under his bed.

— Alethea went to law school hoping that one day she could *mitigate* the world's many injustices.

— Over the years, people of the American southwest have learned how to successfully *mitigate* drought.

modulate

MOJ-uh-leyt **(v.)** to pass from one state to another, especially in music

The photographer's voice began to *modulate* when her camera broke and her *model* was *late*.

— When she picked up the phone, Alicia's voice *modulated* from squeaky and girly to soft and businesslike.

— In the second movement of the concerto, the violins *modulate* from A to A-minor.

— After the family was serenaded with heavy metal music for the twentieth time that night, Dad finally suggested that Kevin *modulate* the volume on his stereo system.

mutable

MYOO-tuh-buhl *(adj.)* able to change

Behold our *mutable mutant bull*!
He sprouts wings and flies when the moon is full.

— April refused to buy high-priced designer clothes because fashion was so *mutable*.
— The classified ad stated that job candidates must be easygoing and *mutable*, due to the demanding and fast-paced nature of the job.
— Far from *mutable*, Jason's cat, Chloe, hid under the bed for a week when he moved to a new apartment.

DRILL 17

Refresh Your Memory

Match the word and link to its corresponding definition.

1. malleable (mallet–able)
2. manifest (Manly Fest)
3. manifold (man, fold)
4. maudlin (Maude in)
5. mawkish (Ma kissed)
6. maxim (mask him)
7. metamorphosis (morph a full size)
8. mitigate (mitts in a gate)
9. modulate (model ... late)
10. mutable (mutant bull)

A. easily understandable, obvious
B. to pass from one state to another, especially in music
C. weakly sentimental
D. diverse, varied
E. characterized by sick sentimentality
F. able to change
G. capable of being shaped or transformed
H. the change of form, shape, substance
I. to make less violent, alleviate
J. a common saying expressing a principle of conduct

Test Your Knowledge

Fill in the blanks with the correct word from the list above. Some word forms may need changing.

1. When I had an awful sore throat, only warm tea would _____ the pain.

2. When I wrote the wrong sum on the chalkboard, my mistake was so _____ that the entire class burst into laughter.

3. Miss Manners's etiquette _____ are both entertaining and instructional.

4. The composer wrote a piece that _____ between minor and major keys.

5. Winnifred went to the gym every day for a year and underwent a _____ from a waiflike girl to an athletic woman.

6. The popularity of Dante's *Inferno* is partly due to the fact that the work allows for _____ interpretations.

7. Although some nineteenth-century critics viewed Dickens's writing as _____ , contemporary readers have found great emotional depth in his works.

8. Because fashion is so _____ , what is trendy today will look outdated in five years.

9. Although many people enjoy romantic comedies, I usually find them _____ and shallow.

10. Maximillian's political opinions were so _____ that anyone he talked to was able to change his mind instantly.

nefarious

ni-FAIR-ee-uhs (*adj.*) heinously villainous

The evil dwarves were quite *nefarious*
when they decided to raid and loot *Ned's fairy house*.

— In the second act, Little Red Riding Hood encounters the
  nefarious wolf.
— During their weekly meeting at the gentlemen's club, the
  mobsters discussed their *nefarious* work.
— The warlock soon returned to his *nefarious* task.

nocturnal

nok-TUR-nl **(adj.)** relating to or occurring
during the night

A _knock turns all_ their heads at night in their beds;
nocturnal sounds fill them with dread.

— To find food in the dark, _nocturnal_ animals have an advanced
sense of sight.
— Rick paid a _nocturnal_ visit to the freezer for a midnight bowl of
ice cream.
— Outside the tent, a _nocturnal_ stillness reigned.

obfuscate

OB-fuh-skeyt **(v.)** **to render incomprehensible, darken**

The sneaky crook had to *obfuscate* the front door's peephole to *rob fussy Kate*.

— Mary-Anne made it a point to *obfuscate* the details of her troubled childhood.

— The sign was *obfuscated* by several large bullet holes.

— Visitors complained that the pamphlet purposefully *obfuscated* the artist's statements.

obscure

uhb-SKYOOR *(adj.)* **unclear, partially hidden**

**Because the sign was *obscure*,
they couldn't know for <u>sure</u> where to turn to get
to shore.**

— The students thought Shakespeare utilized one too many *obscure* turns of phrase.
— Although the hideout was *obscure*, Daniel finally found the stepladder and climbed up to meet the other Treehouse Boys.
— The barista muttered an *obscure* remark before making the triple soy latte.

obsequious

uhb–SEE–kwee–uhs **(adj.)** excessively compliant or submissive

**That rat Maurice is so *obsequious*;
if the boss asks, he'll always _squeak "Yes!"_**

— Before he left the table, the waiter took a deep, *obsequious* bow.
— The assistant's *obsequious* behavior irritated the executive, who occasionally relished a good argument with his underlings.
— Brenda become more *obsequious* when she found out her date was rich.

obstreperous

uhb-STREP-er-uhs (*adj.*) noisy, unruly

**The toddlers at day care were *obstreperous*.
They _obstructed_ our plans and made such a _fuss_!**

- Mrs. Carlisle's first grade class continued to be wild and *obstreperous*, despite her best efforts at discipline.
- The sound coming from the pig barn that morning could only be described as *obstreperous*.
- The *obstreperous* young actresses commanded that their limousine driver run the red light.

onerous

OH-ner-us *(adj.)* burdensome

The forms required were *onerous* when we applied for a loan at *Loans-R-Us*.

— Unprepared in sandals and a T-shirt, Manny found the hike up Mount Washington to be *onerous.*

— Cleaning the barn was Polly's least liked and most *onerous* chore.

— Rachel found babysitting her wild four-year-old brother to be an *onerous* task.

opulent

OP-yuh-luhnt *(adj.)* characterized by rich abundance verging on ostentation

**The _opals_ she _lent_ were _opulent_;
everybody saw them wherever she went.**

— We soon tired of Hollywood, with its *opulent* mansions and manicured lawns.
— On the night of their honeymoon, the newlyweds were presented with the most *opulent* suite in the hotel.
— The CEO preferred to travel in the *opulent* surrounding of his own private jet.

ornate

awr-NEYT (*n.*) highly elaborate, excessively decorated

The other seven trumpets can't compare with *horn eight*— it's made of pure gold, and its design is *ornate*.

— Ophelia's wedding dress was covered in an *ornate* pattern of pearls and lace.

— The seashell's *ornate* swirled pattern mystified the marine biology students.

— Though the church was plain-looking on the outside, the stained glass windows were richly colorful and *ornate*.

ostensible

o-STEN-suh-buhl (*adj.*) appearing as such, seemingly

MC Big Money lived large, *ostensibly*, but in private he invested *sensibly*.

— Claire's *ostensible* aloofness concealed a deep fear of social interaction.
— The corporation's *ostensible* aim was to provide high-quality nutrition to its customers, but it was simply cashing in on a trend labeled "Organic."
— His *ostensible* wealth was belied by a mountain of credit card bills, bounced checks, and promissory notes.

DRILL 18

Refresh Your Memory

Match the word and link to its corresponding definition.

1. nefarious (Ned's fairy house)
2. nocturnal (knock turns all)
3. obfuscate (rob fussy Kate)
4. obscure (sure)
5. obsequious (squeak "Yes!")
6. obstreperous (obstructed ... fuss)
7. onerous (Loans–R–Us)
8. opulent (opals ... lent)
9. ornate (horn eight)
10. ostensible (sensibly)

A. relating to or occurring during the night
B. burdensome
C. highly elaborate, excessively decorated
D. unclear, partially hidden
E. appearing as such, seemingly
F. heinously villainous
G. excessively compliant or submissive
H. noisy, unruly
I. characterized by rich abundance verging on ostentation
J. to render incomprehensible, darken

Test Your Knowledge

Fill in the blanks with the correct word from the list above. Some word forms may need changing.

1. My parents lamented that the pleasures of living in a beautiful country estate no longer outweighed the _____ mortgage payments.

2. The detective did not want to answer the reporter's questions, so he _____ the truth.

3. Mark acted like Janet's servant, obeying her every request in an _____ manner.

4. Although Dr. Meanman's _____ plot to melt the polar icecaps was terrifying, it was so impractical that nobody really worried about it.

5. The _____ styling of the new model of luxury car could not compensate for the poor quality of its motor.

6. Because he was standing in the shadows, his features were _____ .

7. Jackie was a _____ person; she would study until dawn and sleep during the day.

8. Billy's _____ behavior prompted the librarian to ask him to leave the reading room.

9. Jack's _____ reason for driving was that airfare was too expensive, but in reality he was afraid of flying.

10. The _____ furnishings of the dictator's private compound contrasted harshly with the meager accommodations of her subjects.

palliate

PAL-ee-eyt (**v.**) to reduce the severity of

To _palliate_ his insomnia, his _pal Lee ate_ no caffeine, but a pleasant night's sleep still remained to be seen.

— The doctor was able to _palliate_ the infant's symptoms with a small dose of pain medication.

— There was little William could do to _palliate_ the fear and loneliness of his wife's depression.

— The optimistic new mayor hoped to _palliate_ the effects of a brutal police force that had taken over the city.

paragon

PAIR-a-gahn (*n.*) a model of excellence or perfection

Daddy's Little Dentist!

Daddy's Little Dentist!

The dentist's sons had a *paragon* *pair of gums*.

— Miranda thought her brother was the *paragon* of goodwill after she saw him help a little old lady cross the street.

— Always a *paragon* student, Jamie declined the invitation and went home to study for finals.

— The Weir's golden retriever was a *paragon* of obedience after it completed puppy kindergarten.

pariah

puh-RAHY-uh **(n.)** **an outcast**

The mean old *piranha*
was an underwater *pariah*.

— The reporter was treated as a social *pariah* after she wrote a scathing article about the discriminatory rules at the local country club.

— When she returned to work after a nasty case of the flu, Joanna felt like a *pariah*.

— He was the *pariah* of the village, always ignored, or worse, taunted.

partisan

PAHR-tuh-zuhn **(n.)** a follower, adherent

The Italian chef was blatantly *partisan*: All his recipes reflected his love of *parmesan*.

— The Williamstown farmers were angered by *partisans* championing development in their small, rural town.

— Democratic *partisans* rooted exuberantly for their candidate at the rally on the steps of City Hall.

— A *partisan* for the cause, Frank marched and waved flags in every antiwar parade.

penchant

PEN-chuhnt (*n.*) a tendency, partiality, preference

Straight and dull | **Curly and cool**

Penny **didn't care much for straight-haired boys or girls—she pretty much just had a** *penchant* **for curls.**

— Serafina had a *penchant* for guys with long, blond hair.

— Their *penchant* for Ultimate Frisbee lead them to play on opposing teams.

— Mona's *penchant* for pizza was all-consuming: She sampled slices in every state she visited.

pervasive

per–VEY–siv **(adj.)** having the tendency to spread throughout

In the tiny schoolhouse, chicken pox were *pervasive*; **the argument for canceling class was very** *persuasive*.

— Lakshmi tried to avoid consuming corn syrup, but it was a *pervasive* ingredient, found in almost everything.
— His liberal colleagues argued otherwise, but Raul knew first-hand that racism was still *pervasive*.
— The scent of vanilla candles was *pervasive* at the dusty old antique shop.

philanthropic

fil-uhn-THROP-ik (*adj.*) charitable, giving

Scrooge thought he was *philanthropic*, but his gift to Tiny Tim was <u>microscopic</u>.

— The *philanthropic* group contributed more than three million dollars toward the environmental clean-up effort.

— Emily's scholarship was provided by a *philanthropic* educational organization.

— Bill Gates is known for his extensive *philanthropy*, especially in the field of AIDS research and prevention in Africa.

phlegmatic

fleg–MAT–ik *(adj.)* uninterested, unresponsive

On the wild streets of the city, fast-moving people can be *phlegmatic*: ignoring the bustle and *flying legs* is *automatic*.

— After Thanksgiving dinner, everyone felt *phlegmatic* and retired to the couch to watch football.

— So *phlegmatic* were her students, the teacher often wondered whether they were zombies.

— When riding the crosstown bus, Malinda usually put on her most *phlegmatic* facial expression, or else risk communication from strangers.

platitude

PLAT-i-tood (*n.*) an uninspired remark, a cliché

Uncle Murray is an average, _plain dude_, but he speaks in maddening _platitudes_.

— The candidate's speech was overstuffed with *platitudes* and repetitive phrases.
— Darlene found no comfort in her mother's condescending *platitudes*.
— George preferred to utter *platitudes* instead of engaging in any meaningful conversation.

plenitude

PLEN-i-tood **(n.)** an abundance

The *planet dude* had a *plenitude* of alien, outerspace attitude.

— Aunt Bertha's Thanksgiving dinner featured a *plenitude* of Brussels sprouts, much to Michelle's dismay.

— Though he had a *plenitude* of female friends, Mark couldn't decide whom to ask to the dance.

— At first Chelsea thought the cat she adopted was simply fat, but when she discovered a *plenitude* of kittens in her laundry basket one afternoon, she saw otherwise.

DRILL 19

Refresh Your Memory

Match the word and link to its corresponding definition.

1. palliate (pal Lee ate)
2. paragon (pair of gums)
3. pariah (piranha)
4. partisan (parmesan)
5. penchant (Penny)
6. pervasive (persuasive)
7. philanthropic (microscopic)
8. phlegmatic (flying legs ... automatic)
9. platitude (plain dude)
10. plenitude (planet dude)

A. charitable, giving
B. an abundance
C. a tendency, partiality, preference
D. an uninspired remark, a cliché
E. an outcast
F. having the tendency to spread throughout
G. a follower, adherent
H. a model of excellence or perfection
I. to reduce the severity of
J. uninterested, unresponsive

Test Your Knowledge

Fill in the blanks with the correct word from the list above. Some word forms may need changing.

1. Following the discovery of his plagiarism, Professor Hurley was made a _____ in all academic circles.

2. Stepping off the plane in Havana, I recognized the _____ odor of sugar cane fields on fire.

3. My grandmother was overwhelmed by the _____ of tomatoes her garden yielded this season.

4. Jill's dinner parties quickly became monotonous on account of her _____ for Mexican dishes.

5. The doctor trusted that the new medication would _____ her patient's discomfort.

6. Monique feared her dog was ill after the animal's _____ response toward his favorite chew toy.

7. The mythical Helen of Troy was considered a _____ of female beauty.

8. Many people felt that the billionaire's decision to donate her fortune to house the homeless was the ultimate _____ act.

9. The king did not believe that his rival could round up enough _____ to overthrow the monarchy.

10. After reading over her paper, Helene concluded that what she thought were profound insights were actually just _____ .

pliable

PLAHY-uh-buhl (*adj.*) flexible

The on-call giraffe walker was *pleasantly reliable*, because her schedule was so *pliable*.

— The blacksmith heated the iron until it was hot and *pliable*.
— A *pliable* old leather belt hung idly on a hook in the front hallway.
— Years of gymnastics had made Victoria's hamstrings extremely *pliable*.

preponderance

pri-PON-der-uhns (*n.*) superiority in importance or quantity

The tribe was extremely good at their _pond dance_; where there once was no water, now there was a _preponderance_.

— The beach volleyball team had a *preponderance* of blondes, and Olivia felt out of place with her mop of brown hair.

— Ariel liked to believe in the *preponderance* of good over evil, even if on a day-to-day basis it seemed like evil was winning out.

— The overgrown lawn was dominated by a *preponderance* of weeds.

presage

PRES-ij (*n.*) an omen

**The gypsy said the *presage*
contained an ominous *message*.**

— The chief sought a *presage* before declaring war.
— Sarah saw the rainstorm as a *presage* that she shouldn't go for a
  run that day.
— A *presage* indicated that the stocks would not perform as they
  had in the past.

privation

prahy-VEY-shuhn (*n.*) lacking basic necessities

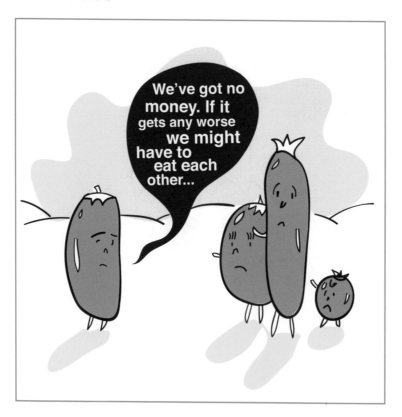

**Living in *privation*,
the tomato family faced *starvation*.**

— After a childhood spent in *privation*, Judah found it difficult to adjust to the presence of typical middle-class luxuries.
— Soldiers in the trenches experienced a life of *privation*.
— Nadja never knew *privation*, but worked hard to prevent it in her community by volunteering at the soup kitchen.

profuse

pruh-FYOOS (*adj.*) plentiful, abundant

**When he missed the goal, the *pro's excuses* were *profuse*:
He said he was distracted and his shoelaces were loose.**

— Aaron's apology was so *profuse* that Carla couldn't help but think
he was apologizing for more than just getting them lost.

— Colonel Franklin wondered why he felt so dizzy, then he noticed
the *profuse* bleeding from his leg.

— The CEO's *profuse* holiday party spending caused some bad
publicity when a picture of an ice sculpture carved in his
likeness appeared in the papers.

proscribe

proh-SKRAHYB **(v.)** to condemn, outlaw

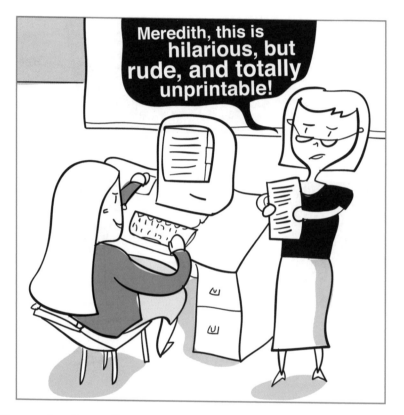

**Although the offensive novelist was a *pro scribe*,
her work was what her editor was paid to *proscribe*.**

— The gaming community *proscribed* certain tactics for being too aggressive.

— Mother *proscribed* the eating of all sugary cereals until we were in our teens.

— The Bible *proscribes* many activities that people today find quite enjoyable.

puerile

PYOOR-ahyl **(adj.)** juvenile, immature

**"*P.U., Riley*! Your *puerile* prank
made a giant mess that really stank!"**

— Stella said she could no longer stand for the *puerile* humor of her
  seven male bandmates.
— After offering a series of *puerile* excuses, David finally admitted
  that he hadn't written the paper.
— His writing was *puerile* and bland, but he was accepted to the
  program because of his connection to an esteemed author.

pulchritude

PUHL–kri-tood **(n.)** physical beauty

Stunned by the body builder's *pulchritude*,
Paula cries, "Dude, **you're so hot, you might get sued."**

— The beauty pageant contestant's radiant *pulchritude* earned her the title of Miss Mississippi.

— Damien loved his wife not only for her *pulchritude* but also for her sharp sense of humor and impeccable taste in wine.

— Rapidly approaching eighty, Gloria spent less and less time gazing in the mirror, no longer concerned about her own *pulchritude*.

punitive

PYOO-ni-tiv *(adj.)* involving punishment

Puny Tiff had a *punitive* streak:
Although she was weak, she punished the meek.

- The general called for *punitive* action against the opposing forces.
- Though she was normally quite liberal, Ellen believed strongly in *punitive* justice.
- Maria's four-inch heels were *punitive*, but they looked great.

quell

kwell **(v.)** to control or diffuse a potentially explosive situation

The good witch will *quell* the bad witch's spell, and now Nell will smell *quite well*.

- The prime minister was unable to *quell* the political upheaval that had swept across the nation.
- A waitress managed to *quell* the rapidly escalating bar fight before anyone called the police.
- Pauline could barely *quell* her anger after yet another man whistled at her on the street.

DRILL 20

Refresh Your Memory

Match the word and link to its corresponding definition.

1. pliable (pleasantly reliable)
2. preponderance (pond dance)
3. presage (message)
4. privation (starvation)
5. profuse (pro's excuses)
6. proscribe (pro scribe)
7. puerile (P.U., Riley)
8. pulchritude (Paula cries, Dude)
9. punitive (puny Tiff)
10. quell (quite well)

A. juvenile, immature
B. superiority in importance or quantity
C. lacking basic necessities
D. physical beauty
E. to control or diffuse a potentially explosive situation
F. plentiful, abundant
G. an omen
H. involving punishment
I. to condemn, outlaw
J. flexible

Test Your Knowledge

Fill in the blanks with the correct word from the list above. Some word forms may need changing.

1. The judge demanded order after the lawyer's _____ attempt to object by stomping his feet on the courtroom floor.

2. When my uncle's old war injury ached, he interpreted it as a _____ of bad weather approaching.

3. The town council voted to _____ the sale of alcohol on weekends.

4. Aircraft wings are designed to be somewhat _____ so they do not break in heavy turbulence.

5. The fans were _____ in their cheers for the star basketball player.

6. The skilled leader deftly _____ the rebellion.

7. Several of Shakespeare's sonnets explore the _____ of a lovely young man.

8. Britain's _____ of naval might secured the nation's role as a military power.

9. After decades of rule by an oppressive government that saw nothing wrong with stealing from its citizens, the recent drought only increased the people's _____ .

10. If caught smoking in the boys' room, the _____ result is immediate expulsion from school.

quixotic

kwik–SOT–ik (*adj.*) idealistic, impractical

"What will you build next with your own two hands sir?"
His *quixotic* answer: "an *exotic* dancer!"

— When the car broke down, the small child offered a series of
  quixotic suggestions on how to fix it.

— Though his ideas were *quixotic*, he had the best intentions.

— Heather had a *quixotic* desire to only eat foods grown within a
  twenty-five-mile radius of her hometown.

recalcitrant

ree-CAL-sih-trant **(adj.)** defiant, unapologetic

"Our son sure was angry and recalcitrant," says Ma, as she _recalls his rant_.

— Bill's _recalcitrant_ attitude earned him a year in military school, where he soon learned to obey authority.

— Though he had a reputation for being cold and _recalcitrant_, Jane found her boss to be funny and easy to work with.

— The _recalcitrant_ group stormed the dean's office and demanded more vegetarian options in the cafeteria.

reconcile

REK-uhn-sahyl   **1. (v.) to return to harmony**
2. (v.) to make consistent with existing ideas

> Kathy! I'm a forgiving person... but why did you crash my car into a tree?!

> I was bored?

Cindy tried to be peaceful and *reconcile*, but her sister's wicked ways would <u>wreck her style</u>.

— Carolyn and her brother eventually *reconciled* after years of avoiding each other.

— Keith finally cracked open his checkbook and attempted to *reconcile* his accounts.

— The arbitrator found it difficult to *reconcile* the union's demands with management's stubbornness.

relegate

REL-i-geyt **1. (v.) to assign to the proper place**
2. (v.) to assign to an inferior place

The lousy cook was *relegated*
to making sure all the carrots were *really grated*.

— After spilling coffee on a manuscript, the intern was *relegated*
to the mail room, where he sorted the incoming mail and made
photocopies for the editors.
— Astronomers recently *relegated* Pluto from planet to dwarf
planet.
— Donald was *relegated* to the advanced math class after acing the
placement test.

replete

ri-PLEET (*adj.*) full, abundant

Arg! No more pleats!

Rita was with anger *replete*
as she *repeated* to the dry cleaner, "No more *pleats*!"

— They found that the pond was *replete* with fish, and gleefully set out to bait their hooks.
— It was perfect beach reading: a novel *replete* with drama, romance, and suspense.
— The local college bar was *replete* with sub-par liquors and cheap, undrinkable beers.

repudiate

ri–PYOO–dee–eyt **(v.) to reject, refuse to accept**

**The critic had to *repudiate* his glowing review;
the _red pudding he ate_ really tasted like glue.**

— It didn't matter that Anita could *repudiate* the charges; the
  senator was too powerful and convicted her in the court of
  public opinion.
— Gerald felt he could *repudiate* his sister's accusation of laziness,
  but he just couldn't bring himself to do it.
— The new president *repudiated* her predecessor's policies by
  freeing all political prisoners.

requisition

rek-wuh-ZISH-uhn (*n.*) a demand for goods, usually made by an authority

The board denied the teacher's paper *requisition*— **saying kids** *wrecked* **her** *quizzes* **was a bad decision!**

— When the army arrived in town, it issued a *requisition* for flour, eggs, and potatoes to be used for the soldiers' rations.

— As hotel manager, I was responsible for making *requisitions* from our vendors.

— The settlers put forth a *requisition* for the natives' corn.

rescind

ri–SIND (*v.*) to take back, repeal

Reggie wished he could *rescind* his recent tendency to *pass wind*.

— The publisher *rescinded* his offer once he saw the book's crude illustrations.

— Despite years of petitioning by the public, City Council may *rescind* the public transportation bill.

— The judge refused to *rescind* the suspension of his driver's license.

respite

RESS-pit (*n.*) a break, rest

Tired Tim took a *respite* from the *chess pit*.

— Olivia needed *respite* after hours of algebra homework.
— The pitcher got his *respite* after the fifth inning.
— The desert's cool oasis was *respite* for the tired camel.

resplendent

ri–SPLEN-duhnt *(adj.)* shiny, glowing

The spoiled redhead loved her rings *resplendent*, but all that sparkling did not help _Red blend in_.

— She held her newborn son and beamed a *resplendent* smile at her husband.
— The meadow outside the farmhouse was *resplendent* with beautiful wildflowers.
— The young actress glided across the red carpet, looking *resplendent* in a glittering gold dress.

DRILL 21

Refresh Your Memory

Match the word and link to its corresponding definition.

1. quixotic (exotic)
2. recalcitrant (recalls his rant)
3. reconcile (wreck her style)
4. relegate (really grated)
5. replete (repeated … pleats)
6. repudiate (red pudding he ate)
7. requisition (wrecked … quizzes)
8. rescind (pass wind)
9. respite (chess pit)
10. resplendent (Red blend in)

A. shiny, glowing
B. to take back, repeal
C. defiant, unapologetic
D. to reject, refuse to accept
E. idealistic, impractical
F. full, abundant
G. a demand for goods, usually made by an authority
H. to return to harmony
I. to assign to an inferior place
J. a break, rest

Test Your Knowledge

Fill in the blanks with the correct word from the list above. Some word forms may need changing.

1. The company _____ its offer of employment after discovering that Jane's resume was full of lies.

2. During the war, the government made a _____ of supplies.

3. The feuding neighbors finally _____ when one brought the other a delicious tuna noodle casserole.

4. The partygoers were _____ in diamonds and fancy dress.

5. Kwame made a strong case for an extension of his curfew, but his mother _____ it with a few biting words.

6. Edward entertained a _____ desire to fall in love at first sight in a laundromat.

7. After spilling a drink on a customer's shirt, the waiter found himself _____ to the least lucrative shift.

8. Justin left the pub to gain a brief _____ from the smoke and noise.

9. Even when scolded, the _____ young girl simply stomped her foot and refused to finish her lima beans.

10. The unedited version was _____ with naughty words.

ribald

RIB-uhld (*adj.*) coarsely, crudely humorous

**It was *ribald* for Dan
to *rib* the *bald* man.**

— The child recited a *ribald* limerick at the dinner table and was promptly grounded by his parents.
— Derek endured several *ribald* comments after announcing to his friends that he and his wife were expecting a baby.
— The dentist's *ribald* sense of humor infuriated his receptionist.

salient

SEY-lee-uhnt *(adj.)* significant, conspicuous

Sail entirely around the *salient* peak—
then you'll find the treasure you seek.

— A brief outline covered all the *salient* points of the four hundred-page document.

— Unfortunately, her most *salient* traits were also her worst: She was loud, and constantly interrupted people in conversation.

— There are a few *salient* differences between digital and traditional photography, one of which is the use of film.

sanguine

SANG-gwin **(adj.)** optimistic, cheery

"Come back to me, sweet Stewart," <u>*sang Gwen*</u>**,
who was *sanguine* and knew it was a matter of when.**

— After the accident, no one appreciated Jeff's *sanguine*
  exclamation that things could only get better.
— Maura was glad to be mother to a *sanguine*, giggling baby.
— She had *sanguine* expectations about her blind date, and was
  bitterly disappointed when they finally met.

scintillating

SIN-til-eyt-ing **(adj.)** sparkling

**The boys have to _stay till eight_
to see the comets _scintillate_.**

— Bernardo's eyes were a pale, clear blue marked by _scintillating_
flecks of green and gold.
— The entire galaxy seemed to _scintillate_ in the sky before her.
— Known for her _scintillating_ wit, Kerry was a natural fit for the
editorial board of the humor magazine.

scrupulous

SKROO-pyuh-luhs **(v.) painstaking, careful**

**The ice cream man is *scrupulous*—
if you want it small, he'll *scoop you less*.**

— Edna's *scrupulous* research on native Kentucky grasses won her a grant for further study.
— The surgeon sewed up the wound with a *scrupulous* attention to detail.
— Jaqueline was *scrupulous* about cleaning the bathroom and scrubbed each crack with an old toothbrush.

serene

SUH-reen **(*adj.*) calm, untroubled**

The ocean <u>scene</u> was *serene*;
no waves were seen.

— Looking for a place for a picnic, Kimberly and Brian chose a patch of grass next to a *serene* lake.

— Wilma smiled *serenely* as the sun set over the water.

— Practicing Zen meditation always gave Priya a sense of *serenity*.

solvent

SOL-vuhnt **1. (*n.*) a substance that can dissolve other substances**
2. (*adj.*) able to pay debts, expand

"I've *solved it*!" said brainy Alexei, but then his *solvent* exploded all over again.

— Wesley vowed he would move out of his parents' house as soon as he was financially *solvent*.

— The *solvent* easily removed the gum from Jane's hair, but unfortunately it removed her hair, too.

— The directions said to mix the sugar into its *solvent*, milk, and let it sit for five minutes.

somnolent

SOM-nuh-luhnt **(adj.)** sleepy, drowsy

**Sophie wasn't _somnolent_, though it was time for bed,
so her _son lent_ her a sleeping pill and soon
she slept like the dead.**

— After the six-hour car ride, Abby felt _somnolent_ and went
straight to bed.
— The 7:30 A.M. math class often left James _somnolent_, and he
struggled to keep from nodding off.
— After a long game of fetch, the _somnolent_ puppy finally fell
asleep in its owner's lap.

speculative

SPEK-yuh-ley-tiv **(adj.)** not based in fact

Cousin Gerald
(no glasses)

Cousin Gerald
(glasses)

Cousin Gerald claims he's my _cute relative_,
but when he wears his _specs_, that seems _speculative_.

— They took a _speculative_ gold-digging trip to the foothills of southwestern New Mexico.

— Calvin's knowledge about gardening was purely _speculative_, but he couldn't refrain from making suggestions as his wife pulled the weeds.

— When her boyfriend stopped returning her calls, Patrice came to the _speculative_ conclusion that he was cheating on her.

staid

steyd *(adj.)* sedate, serious, self-restrained

The *staid* _maid_ never, ever played.

— A *staid* and sober man, the father refused to play charades with his family.
— Once she was freed from the *staid* confines of boarding school, Lisa began her wild summer adventures.
— Compared with today, the world of the early 1900s seems *staid* and boring.

DRILL 22

Refresh Your Memory

Match the word and link to its corresponding definition.

1. ribald (rib ... bald)
2. salient (sail around)
3. sanguine (sang Gwen)
4. scintillating (stay till eight)
5. scrupulous (scoop you less)
6. serene (scene)
7. solvent (solved it)
8. somnolent (son lent)
9. speculative (specs ... cute relative)
10. staid (maid)

A. sedate, serious, self-restrained
B. sparkling
C. a substance that can dissolve other substances
D. significant, conspicuous
E. sleepy, drowsy
F. optimistic, cheery
G. painstaking, careful
H. coarsely, crudely humorous
I. calm, untroubled
J. not based in fact

Test Your Knowledge

Fill in the blanks with the correct word from the list above. Some word forms may need changing.

1. The _____ student kept falling asleep and waking up with a jerk.

2. Water is sometimes called the universal _____ because almost all other substances can dissolve into it.

3. Polly reacted to any bad news with a _____ smile and the chirpy cry, "When life hands you lemons, make lemonade!"

4. Louise stood in front of the Mona Lisa, puzzling over the famous woman's _____ smile.

5. While some giggled at the _____ joke involving a parson's daughter, most sighed and rolled their eyes.

6. One of the _____ differences between Alison and Nancy is that Alison is a foot taller.

7. With _____ care, Sam cut a snowflake out of white paper.

8. The _____ butler never changed his expression no matter what happened.

9. The ice skater's _____ rhinestone costume nearly blinded the judges.

10. Sadly, Tessa was convicted on merely _____ evidence.

stingy

STIN-jee **(*adj.*) not generous, not inclined to spend or give**

"Mom," said the robot child, "don't be so *stingy*! My old pants are rusty; please buy me new _tin jeans_!"

— Susanne was *stingy* with her affection—she permitted her boyfriend no more than a hug on weeknights.

— His children thought he was *stingy*, but Leonard preferred to think of himself as frugal.

— Gordon thought his company's one-week annual vacation package was *stingy*, so he called in sick once a month.

sublime

suh–BLAHYM *(adj.)* lofty, grand, exalted

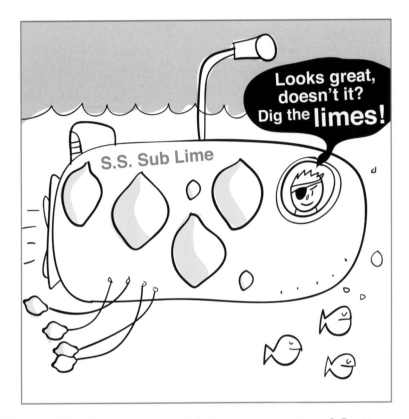

**Crazy Carl decorated his new <u>sub</u> with <u>limes</u>.
To most it looked nuts, but to him it's *sublime*.**

— The *sublime* writings of John Milton were the subject of Henry's
  dissertation.
— Gregory hoped to apply the philosopher's *sublime* teachings to
  his plain and simple life.
— The summer's *sublime* heirloom tomatoes appear in markets in
  August.

tacit

TAS-it (*adj.*) expressed without words

The receiver's signal was *tacit*,
so the quarterback knew when to *pass it*.

— Jake took his mother's lack of conversation on the matter as *tacit* approval that he could attend the rock concert.

— With a *tacit* smile, the two lovers agreed to elope under cover of night.

— Every night, Margaret offered a *tacit* prayer for world peace.

tenuous

TEN-yoo-uhs **(adj.)** having little substance or strength

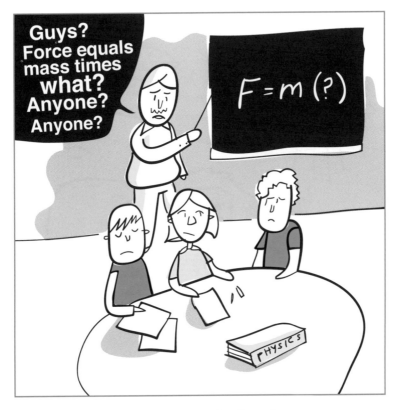

Our study group's grasp of physics was *tenuous*, so we hired a tutor to *tend to us*.

— The scientist's theory was *tenuous*, at best, yet it somehow held up in his first experiment.

— Ruthie clung desperately to her *tenuous* belief in Santa Claus well into her teens.

— The link between childhood trauma and adult neurosis is *tenuous*, but it is nevertheless frequently explored by amateur psychologists.

terrestrial

tuh-RES-tree-uhl **(*adj.*) relating to the land**

**The alien explorers weren't *terrestrial*,
but the lion still found them *digestible*.**

— A scientific panel agreed that the *terrestrial* ecosystem had been
  disrupted by carbon emissions.
— The *terrestrial* plants suffered when they were moved to a
  watery environment.
— Pilar thought of herself as *terrestrial*; she had a strong feeling for
  the earth, and was a successful gardener.

timorous

TIM-er-uhs **(adj.)** timid, fearful

The employees were angry and no longer *timorous*.
They threatened to quit, saying "It's *Tim or us***!"**

— His voice was *timorous* and his face pale as he and his friends
approached the haunted house.
— Julia stepped onstage with a *timorous* shudder and vowed to
remember her lines.
— Around other dogs, the *timorous* puppy cowered and yelped.

tome

tohm (*n.*) a large book

The tiny *gnome*
read a giant *tome*.

— The dusty *tome* had become a permanent fixture on his desk, like an overgrown paperweight.

— Stuffed with various pre-med *tomes*, Renee's backpack very likely outweighed her.

— Perched on a pedestal in the corner of the library with an old magnifying glass at its side, the unabridged dictionary seemed an imposing *tome*.

torrid

TOR-id *(adj.)* giving off intense heat, passionate

Summer days can be *torrid*,
and the smells they raise are truly *horrid*.

— Locked in a *torrid* embrace in the backseat of their car, the young lovers failed to see a police officer step up beside the window.

— Emily's preferred beach reading featured *torrid* romances between long-haired maidens and muscular cowboys.

— The *torrid* mid-July afternoon sapped all the energy out of Kathleen's body.

tortuous

TAWR-choo-uhs *(adj.)* winding

The _tortoise_ asked directions of a passing toad— he was always getting lost on the *tortuous* road.

- From the observation deck, she could see the *tortuous* path leading down into the Grand Canyon.
- The farmer wasn't sure if the old truck would make it over the rough, *tortuous* roads.
- Frank succumbed to motion sickness after a long ride on a beautiful but *tortuous* coastal highway.

tractable

TRAK-tuh-buhl **(*adj.*) easily controlled**

Tractable **Tim's face was grim,
as he handed control of the *track table* over to Slim.**

— Samantha's unwieldy poodle was finally *tractable* after a year of positive training.

— Whenever the babysitter mentioned ice cream, the children immediately became *tractable*.

— Under the watch of his supervisor, Scott was meek and *tractable*.

DRILL 23

Refresh Your Memory

Match the word and link to its corresponding definition.

1. stingy (tin jeans)
2. sublime (sub ... limes)
3. tacit (pass it)
4. tenuous (tend to us)
5. terrestrial (digestible)
6. timorous (Tim or us)
7. tome (gnome)
8. torrid (horrid)
9. tortuous (tortoise)
10. tractable (track table)

A. timid, fearful
B. relating to the land
C. easily controlled
D. not generous, not inclined to spend or give
E. giving off intense heat, passionate
F. lofty, grand, exalted
G. a large book
H. expressed without words
I. having little substance or strength
J. winding

Test Your Knowledge

Fill in the blanks with the correct word from the list above. Some word forms may need changing.

1. I didn't want to witness the neighbor's _____ affair through the window.

2. In college, I used to carry around an anatomy book that was the heaviest _____ in my bag.

3. The homeless man sadly pondered his former wealth and once- _____ existence.

4. Elephants are _____ animals.

5. I interpreted my parents' refusal to talk as a _____ acceptance of my request.

6. Scrooge's _____ habits did not fit with the generous, giving spirit of Christmas.

7. When dealing with the unknown, _____ Tallulah almost always broke down in tears.

8. The scary thing about driving in mountains are the narrow, _____ roads.

9. Your argument is very _____ , since it relies so much on speculation and hearsay.

10. The horse was so _____ , Myra didn't even need a bridle.

tremulous

TREM-yuh-luhs **(v.)** fearful

**Tristan's tightrope walk was truly *tremulous*:
He's what the circus folk would call a <u>trembling wuss</u>.**

— Her voice was *tremulous* as she called, through the blackness of her house, "Who's there?"
— Movies about deep sea exploration always made Marty *tremulous*—he didn't like thinking about the kinds of creatures that might lurk down there.
— The kindergarteners huddled in a *tremulous* mass outside the classroom door on the first day of school.

truncate

TRUHNG-keyt **(v.)** to shorten by cutting off

**Don't try to _truncate_ an elephant's _trunk_.
It might put him in a terrible funk.**

— Their three o'clock water-cooler conversation was _truncated_ by the arrival of the boss.
— The instructions were _truncated_ because of a printer error, so Amy was unable to make the recipe.
— The numerical value of pi is often _truncated_ to 3.14.

ubiquitous

yoo-BIK-wi-tuhs **(adj.)** existing everywhere, widespread

Keep all the fruit _you pick with us_ — this season's apples are _ubiquitous_.

— The establishment's green signs were _ubiquitous_, beckoning to coffee drinkers and laptop-toting students from nearly every city block.

— Within an hour _ubiquitous_ tiny ants were crawling over every last morsel of the picnic food.

— Corey believed that God was _ubiquitous_, watching over her every move and offering an approving nod every once in a while.

upbraid

uhp-BREYD **(v.)** to criticize or scold severely

If the town isn't burned, then looted and *raided*, the Viking king will make sure his hordes are *upbraided*.

— The captain *upbraided* his crew when they failed to report the approaching submarine.

— In her memoirs, the writer *upbraids* her friends and family for failing to support her when she was suffering from clinical depression.

— Ben's parents *upbraided* him for his dishonesty.

utopia

KAT-l-ahyz **(*n.*) an imaginary and remote place of perfection**

**Frank thinks Hawaii's a *utopia*,
so he told Francine, "It's where I will _elope with ya_."**

— As a child, Catherine often daydreamed about a *utopia* filled with lush green grass and galloping unicorns.

— The beautiful island of Kauai, with its bright flora and lush green foliage, is like a *utopia*.

— In high school, we imagined college would be *utopia*, but we were disappointed to discover that it required hard work.

vacillate

VAS-uh-leyt **(*v.*)** to fluctuate, hesitate

**Lizzie *vacillates* between dates;
she just can't choose between her *very silly mates*.**

— His love for pizza *vacillates* depending on how much beer he has had to drink.
— The water level in Roosevelt lake *vacillates* during dry season.
— Kendall usually wakes up early, but the time can *vacillate* depending on when he went to sleep the night before.

venerable

VEN-er-uh-buhl **(adj.)** deserving of respect
because of age or achievement

Lost in
a swordfight.

Lost throwing
a grenade
out of a tank.

Lost in
a bar bet.

General Bly is a *venerable* guy—
in the war he lost an arm, a leg, and an eye.

— Thomas was nervous about introducing the *venerable*
  congressman.
— The *venerable* news organization now faces possible dissolution
  due to financial difficulties.
— When the *venerable* chief enters the room, papers soon stop
  rustling and all conversation comes to a quick halt.

vicarious

vahy-KAIR-ee-uhs **(adj.) experiencing through another**

When mellow Mary drives *Vic's car with us*, she feels Vic's power, however *vicarious*.

— While her sister cried over a bad breakup, Melissa thought she could almost feel a *vicarious* heartache.
— The young film buff enjoyed *vicarious* thrills while watching his heroes on the big screen.
— Jo remarked that she'd have to experience the rollercoaster *vicariously*: by watching her friends ride it.

vilify

VIL-uh-fahy **(n.) lower in importance, defame**

**Nasty Viv was the _village fiend_,
and the cops _vilified_ her when she split the scene.**

— The supermarket tabloids _vilified_ the young star and her much older lover.
— A letter in the local paper _vilified_ neighborhood teenagers, blaming them for a recent crime spree that left the library vandalized.
— Gregory _vilified_ his ex-girlfriend so vehemently that his friends couldn't help but wonder what had happened between them.

vindictive

vin-DIK-tiv (*adj.*) vengeful

**The pirate's acts were *vindictive*:
He stole *vinegar, dictated* orders,
and didn't let his enemies *live*.**

— The cruel and *vindictive* czar sent the artist to Siberia for painting an unflattering portrait.

— Steven was so *vindictive* that he punched his ex-wife's new husband at her wedding.

— The *vindictive* teacher gave Chris a hard time just because his older brother was a troublemaker.

DRILL 24

Refresh Your Memory

Match the word and link to its corresponding definition.

1. tremulous (trembling wuss)
2. truncate (trunk)
3. ubiquitous (you pick with us)
4. upbraid (raided)
5. utopia (elope with ya)
6. vacillate (very silly mates)
7. venerable (General Bly)
8. vicarious (Vic's car with us)
9. vilify (village fiend)
10. vindictive (vinegar, dictated ... live)

A. an imaginary and remote place of perfection
B. existing everywhere, widespread
C. to lower in importance, defame
D. to fluctuate, hesitate
E. to shorten by cutting off
F. to criticize or scold severely
G. vengeful
H. experiencing through another
I. fearful
J. deserving of respect because of age or achievement

Test Your Knowledge

Fill in the blanks with the correct word from the list above. Some word forms may need changing.

1. My brother learned to be social through _____ involvement in my amazing experiences.

2. After winning the derby, the jockey _____ the long speech he had planned and thanked only his mom and his horse.

3. The last thing I wanted was for Lisa to _____ me again about missing the rent payment.

4. The _____ madman seeks to exact vengeance for any insult that he perceives is directed at him, no matter how small.

5. I always feel a trifle _____ when walking through a graveyard.

6. I prefer a definite answer, but my boss kept _____ between the distinct options available to us.

7. It seems that everyone in the United States has a television. The technology is _____ here.

8. After the Watergate scandal, almost any story written about President Nixon sought to _____ him and criticize his behavior.

9. Everyone in the world wants to live in a _____ , but no one can agree upon the way in which to build one.

10. The _____ Supreme Court justice had made several key rulings in landmark cases throughout the years.

virtuoso

vur-choo-OH-so (*n.*) one who excels in an art; a highly skilled musical performer

Vern the yo-yo virtuoso, **you have to admit it, is so good if he shoots the moon, he'll hit it.**

— By the age of fourteen, he was already a piano *virtuoso*.
— Though everyone was impressed by his guitar-playing skill, Adam didn't consider himself a *virtuoso*.
— The critic glowingly described the artist as a painting *virtuoso*.

vivacious

vi–VEY–shuhs **(adj.)** lively, sprightly

**The cheater was so wound up and *vivacious*
that the table was <u>*vicious*</u> and not very spacious.**

— The *vivacious* toddler was too much for his babysitter, so she
  called her mother for backup.
— Bluebeard tried to kill Blackbeard with a poisoned ale, but it
  only made him more angry and *vivacious*!
— The sandwich that Carlos dropped behind the refrigerator soon
  aquired a thick growth of *vivacious* mold.

vocation

voh–KEY–shuhn **(n.) the work in which someone is employed, profession**

Ave Maria!

**Jenny is a singer and great at her _vocation_:
She perfects any form of _vocal action_.**

— Brandon was able to abide by the complicated office rules because he loved his _vocation_.

— At a party, an attractive young businessman asked the student about her _vocation_, and she stammered out something about being involved in academia.

— Her _vocation_ as a poet often demanded late nights over steaming cups of tea.

wane

weyn **(*v.*) to decrease in size, dwindle**

**The sunshine *waned*
as it rained and *rained*.**

— The moon *waned* in the sky until it was nothing more than a tiny white sliver.
— As his popularity *waned*, the president's speeches grew increasingly desperate.
— Erin ignored her mother's *waning* influence and got a tattoo.

wanton

WAHN-ton **(adj.)** undisciplined, lewd, lustful

**Barry sounded *wanton*
when he asked if the woman might *want one*.**

— Environmentalists warned about the *wanton* depletion of oil reserves, but the president refused to listen.

— The *wanton* child tossed his crayons carelessly across the room.

— The adult store had a *wanton* display in its window.

wizened

WIZ-uhnd *(adj.)* dry, shrunken, wrinkled

The *wizened* wizard
had skin like a lizard.

— After a four-day climb, they reached the summit and a *wizened* old man pointed them toward the Temple of the Jewels.

— Julia considered her grandmother beautiful, though her features were *wizened* and her hair thin and flat.

— Along the shore grew a thick patch of *wizened* brambles that threatened to scrape unprotected ankles.

wrath

rath **(v.)** vengeful anger, punishment

**Benny did not expect his neighbors' *wrath*
when he decided to clean himself in their *birdbath*.**

— She shrunk in her seat, hoping to avoid her professor's *wrath*.

— Although he was livid, Marcus kept his *wrath* concealed and asked sweetly if Annemarie would like another cup of tea.

— My father's *wrath* was well-known in our small apartment building, mostly because almost everyone could hear his angry, bellowing shouts.

zealous

ZEL-uhs **(*adj.*) fervent, filled with eagerness in pursuit of something**

As a marketing exec, our mother's rather *zealous*; why just the other day she even tried to *sell us*!

- *Zealous* in their pursuit of the perfect French fry, the old college friends drove down the California coast, stopping at every roadside burger joint.
- The police force *zealously* enforced the new law against jaywalking, ticketing hundreds of pedestrians.
- The *zealous* football fans chanted furiously as the clock ticked off the final seconds of the game.

zephyr

ZEH-fer (*n.*) a gentle breeze

**The _zany_ butterfly soon _left her_
when it was carried away on a zephyr.**

— A zephyr brushed Bonnie's hair off her neck.
— The young lovers lay in the meadow and felt a zephyr
on their faces.
— Adam needed more than a zephyr to get his kite in the air.

zenith

ZEE-nith *(adj.)* the highest point, culminating point

Winnie described her fast as a spiritual *zenith*, but Tom thought she was deluded by a crazy *Zen myth*.

— The precocious young poet reached her *zenith* at age sixteen, after which her poetry worsened considerably.
— As CEO of a small technology company, Thomas was at the *zenith* of his career.
— The view stretched for miles from the mountain's *zenith*.

DRILL 25

Refresh Your Memory

Match the word and link to its corresponding definition.

1. virtuoso (Vern the yo-yo)
2. vivacious (vicious)
3. vocation (vocal action)
4. wane (rained)
5. wanton (want one)
6. wizened (wizard)
7. wrath (birdbath)
8. zealous (sell us)
9. zephyr (zany ... left her)
10. zenith (Zen myth)

A. dry, shrunken, wrinkled
B. undisciplined, lewd, lustful
C. one who excels in an art; a highly skilled musical performer
D. vengeful anger, punishment
E. a gentle breeze
F. the work in which someone is employed, profession
G. the highest point, culminating point
H. lively, sprightly
I. fervent, filled with eagerness in pursuit of something
J. to decrease in size, dwindle

Test Your Knowledge

Fill in the blanks with the correct word from the list above.
Some word forms may need changing.

1. If he were any more _____ about getting his promotion, he'd practically live at the office.

2. Don't be so afraid of his wrath, because his influence with the president is already beginning to _____ .

3. Did you really want to incur her _____ when she is known for inflicting the worst punishments legally possible?

4. The _____ clown makes all of the children laugh and giggle with his funny antics.

5. I was too nice to tell Nelly that she had reached the absolute _____ of her career with that one hit of hers.

6. Vicky's _____ demeanor often made the frat guys next door very excited.

7. Pat's grandma, Rose, had the most _____ countenance, full of leathery wrinkles.

8. If not for the _____ that were cooling us, our room would've been unbearably hot.

9. Even though Lydia has studied piano for many years, she's only average at it. She's no _____ , that's for sure.

10. After growing tired of the superficial world of high-fashion, Edwina decided to devote herself to a new _____ : social work.

About the Authors

Frances Duncan and **Dan O. Williams** are both artists and writers, as their projects and whims dictate. In this case, Frances wrote the words and Dan drew the cartoons. It could easily have been reversed. They are the proud parents of a lazy marshmallow-colored Labrador retriever, and they live in northwestern Massachusetts.